Praise for
Praying for Your Husband from Head to Toe

"I have never seen a more practical book on how to pray for your husband than *Praying for Your Husband from Head to Toe*. Sharon Jaynes has done wives (and husbands) a great service by writing this book. I can't wait to see what will happen to husbands whose wives choose this challenge to pray."
—GARY CHAPMAN, PHD, author of *The Five Love Languages*

"In this much-needed book, Sharon Jaynes gives readers the whys, whats, and how-tos of praying for a husband. The thirty-day guide for covering every aspect of a man's life through prayer is every wife's dream come true. What a gift! As Sharon writes, 'Prayer can change everything'!"
—ELIZABETH GEORGE, author of *A Woman After God's Own Heart*

"You will be delightfully surprised by the power of this book. Most of us have prayed for our husbands for years, but Sharon's approach is so unique, it will change how we pray for our men forever."
—SHAUNTI FELDHAHN, author of *For Women Only*

"Sharon Jaynes has combined powerful prayers with a practical plan that wives everywhere can follow. Her words are full of wisdom, encouragement, and truth. This book is an invitation to deepen your intimacy with Jesus in ways that will ultimately bless your marriage as well."
—HOLLEY GERTH, author of *You're Already Amazing*

"Every wife wants to know the best way to encourage and support her husband. The best place to begin is by having a conversation with the God who created him. God knows every detail about your husband—his struggles, his concerns, his joys, his fears, his hopes, and his dreams. After all, it's God who wired your husband exactly the way he is. Sharon Jaynes invites you to pray for your husband by releasing the creation (your husband) back to his Creator (our gracious God) and praying for your husband from head to toe each day. This collection of prayers will be an encouragement to your husband, and in the process, you'll be drawn closer to God."
—DIEDRA RIGGS, managing editor of TheHighCalling.org

"Sharon Jaynes has written a book every woman needs on her bedside table. *Praying for Your Husband from Head to Toe* is a powerful and practical marriage changer. A woman will get in tune with God's heart for her husband—and also with herself, her life, and the future blessings and *best* God has for her love."

—PAM FARREL, coauthor of *Men Are Like Waffles—Women Are Like Spaghetti*

"*Praying for Your Husband from Head to Toe* could not have arrived at a more perfect time. With life moving ahead at a near-frantic pace while I attempt—in vain—to keep up, this book is a reminder to slow it all down. My husband needs not only my love, encouragement, and support but most important, my prayers. And not just any boilerplate prayer, but specific prayers over every square inch of his body, mind, and even his sexuality (one of my personal favorites!)."

—FAWN WEAVER, founder of HappyWivesClub.com

"In the nineteen years I've been married to my best friend, I've lived the 'for better or for worse' part of my wedding vows. I've learned so much and assembled quite the tool belt in my journey to love and honor my husband. But nothing—*nothing*—has been as powerful as bowing my heart and knee and simply praying for him. *Praying for Your Husband from Head to Toe* is a practical, powerful guide for blessing not only your spouse's life but also your own. This resource will take your marriage to a new level!"

—KRISTEN WELCH, author of *We Are THAT Family* blog

"One of the most important things we can do as wives is to pray daily for our husbands. Sharon Jaynes has given us a great resource to cover every aspect of our husbands' lives and character with Scripture-based prayer over the course of thirty days. This will be a book I keep on my nightstand for years to come!"

—MELANIE SHANKLE, author of *Sparkly Green Earrings* and TheBigMamaBlog.com

Praying for Your Husband from Head to Toe

Praying for
Your Husband
from Head to Toe

A Daily Guide to Scripture-Based Prayer

Sharon Jaynes

MULTNOMAH
BOOKS

PRAYING FOR YOUR HUSBAND FROM HEAD TO TOE
PUBLISHED BY MULTNOMAH BOOKS
12265 Oracle Boulevard, Suite 200
Colorado Springs, Colorado 80921

All Scripture quotations, unless otherwise indicated, are taken from the Holy Bible, New International Version®, NIV®. Copyright © 1973, 1978, 1984 by Biblica Inc.™ Used by permission of Zondervan. All rights reserved worldwide. www.zondervan.com. Scripture quotations marked (AMP) are taken from the Amplified Bible. Copyright © 1954, 1958, 1962, 1964, 1965, 1987 by The Lockman Foundation. Used by permission. Scripture quotations marked (NASB) are taken from the New American Standard Bible®. © Copyright The Lockman Foundation 1960, 1962, 1963, 1968, 1971, 1972, 1973, 1975, 1977, 1995. Used by permission. (www.Lockman.org). Scripture quotations marked (NCV) are taken from the New Century Version®. Copyright © 1987, 1988, 1991 by Thomas Nelson Inc. Used by permission. All rights reserved. Scripture quotations marked (NKJV) are taken from the New King James Version®. Copyright © 1982 by Thomas Nelson Inc. Used by permission. All rights reserved. Scripture quotations marked (NLT) are taken from the Holy Bible, New Living Translation, copyright © 1996, 2004, 2007. Used by permission of Tyndale House Publishers Inc., Carol Stream, Illinois 60188. All rights reserved.

Italics in Scripture quotations reflect the author's added emphasis.

Hardcover ISBN 978-1-60142-471-6
eBook ISBN 978-1-60142-472-3

Cover design by Mark D. Ford
Cover photo by Reggie Casagrande, The Image Bank/Getty Images

Published in the United States by WaterBrook Multnomah, an imprint of the Crown Publishing Group, a division of Random House LLC, New York, a Penguin Random House Company.

MULTNOMAH and its mountain colophon are registered trademarks of Random House LLC.

The Cataloging-in-Publication Data is on file with the Library of Congress.

Printed in the United States of America
2013—First Edition

10 9 8 7 6 5 4 3 2 1

SPECIAL SALES
Most WaterBrook Multnomah books are available at special quantity discounts when purchased in bulk by corporations, organizations, and special-interest groups. Custom imprinting or excerpting can also be done to fit special needs. For information, please e-mail SpecialMarkets @WaterBrookMultnomah.com or call 1-800-603-7051.

Dedicated to my husband, Steve,
the man who captured my heart the first time I laid eyes
on him over three decades ago.

CONTENTS

Part 1

The Power and Purpose
of Prayer

I can still remember being sequestered in the "bride's room" of our church just moments before the organist began to play for the early arrivals. As I sat in front of an oversized gilded mirror, trying not to wrinkle my dress, I daydreamed about the man who would become my husband by day's end. He was everything I had ever hoped for: handsome, smart, ambitious, and strong. And most important, he had a deeply intimate relationship with Jesus.

My delicate white gown fit snugly around my upper frame, and a flowing satin train trailed behind. A veil rested on a nearby table, ready to be positioned on my head. My bouquet of white roses stood at attention, waiting to be placed in my hands. The most important people in my life gathered in the sanctuary to witness the "I do's."

Yes, this was a good day.

As I stared at my reflection, my heart so full of hope and promise, an unwelcome thought interrupted my musing. *Doesn't every woman feel this way on her wedding day? What could go so terribly wrong that such a high percentage of marriages end in divorce? Am I fooling myself? Am I that much different from the thousands who have walked the aisle before me?*

I decided right then and there that I would do everything in my power to make my marriage a success. It didn't take long for me to discover that the words *in my power* were a problem. "My power" was not enough.

Fairy tales always end with the words "And they lived happily ever after." But if we could read the epilogue to those rides off into the sunset, we'd most likely find daily struggles, potentially divisive decisions, and angry arguments sprinkled throughout. Fairy tales stop short of telling us about tension over whose turn it is to wash the dishes, pay the bills, or put the kids to bed. They leave out the part about stress over holidays with in-laws, frequency of intimacy, and who gets to spend what when. We naively repeat the words "for better or for worse" and then are shocked when the first hint of "worse" rears its ugly head.

Prayer Can Change Everything

If you've been married for more than a few days, then you have most likely figured out that the blessed union doesn't stay so blessed without a lot of work. And I dare say, the most important "work" we can do as wives is on our knees. The psalmist wrote, "Unless the LORD builds the house, its builders labor in vain. Unless the LORD watches over the city, the watchmen stand guard in vain" (Psalm 127:1). Only God can truly protect your marriage and your man. And He invites you to participate in the unleashing of His power by praying for your husband and turning the key to the storehouse of heaven's door for blessings outpoured.

Louise saw this happen with her husband, Allan, in a miraculous way.

Allan was a tough man. Raised by a single mom with five siblings during the Depression in the early 1930s, Allan learned how to scrap his way through life and climb to the top of humanity's heap through sheer determination and grit. He married at nineteen, had his first son at twenty, then a baby girl at twenty-five. Over the next two decades he advanced from driving a delivery truck at a lumberyard to becoming part owner and president of a building supply company in eastern North Carolina.

Allan drank heavily, fought with his wife physically, and terrorized his children emotionally. He gambled, dabbled in pornography, and had questionable relationships laced with a host of unsavory vices. But when his teenage daughter became a Christian and began praying for her family, God grabbed the chisel of grace and began chipping away at Allan's proud heart of stone. Three years after his daughter's decision to follow Christ, his wife, Louise, became a believer as well. His wife, his daughter, and a host of other prayer warriors began interceding with God on Allan's behalf.

When Allan was forty-six years old, his life took several hairpin twists and troublesome turns. Because of a business deal gone terribly wrong, he was sued for breach of contract for breaking a noncompete clause with a former employer. Fearing exposure in court and, more important, in his small community, Allan teetered on the brink of a nervous breakdown. From man's perspective, it appeared he was on the verge of losing it all. From God's perspective, Allan was right where he needed to be.

One day, in a surge of panic, Allan drove home from work, only to remember his wife was at a meeting in Pennsylvania. He got back in his car and drove five hundred miles to try and find her. As he drove into the town where he expected to find his wife, he passed a church. Immediately, Allan made a U-turn, parked his car, and ran inside the ornate building.

"Excuse me, ma'am," he said with tears in his eyes. "I need someone to pray for me. Is the preacher available? I need help."

"I'm sorry, sir," the church receptionist said. "He's not in, but I know a man who can help you. Here," she said as she sketched out directions on a scrap of paper. "The pastor of the Baptist church down the street is out doing some construction work on their new church building. Why don't you drive on over there? I bet he can help you."

So Allan got back in his car, followed the receptionist's crude map, and found the country preacher out in the woods working on his church. With a hammer in his hand and Jesus in his heart, the pastor turned to Allan and asked, "What can I do for you?"

"I need you to pray for me," Allan explained as tears ran down his weathered cheeks.

"Let's sit down on this log while you tell me what's going on."

For several hours Allan sat with a fellow builder and told him all he had ever done. When he had finished his confession, the pastor put his arm around this broken man and said, "Now, Allan, let me tell you what I've done."

The way Allan later explained it, "I told this man everything I had ever done. Then he told me he had done the very same things. And I knew if God could forgive him, and he could be a preacher, then God could forgive me too."

Allan knelt in the woods of Pennsylvania with angels hovering low. Heaven's host celebrated as he gave his heart to Christ and made Jesus the Lord of his life. "Amazing grace, how sweet the sound…" But for me, this is more than a *sweet* story. It is a miraculous memory. Allan was my dad.

From my earliest years as a Christian, I experienced the power of prayer to change a man's life—to strengthen a man's resolve, to protect a man's heart, and to mature a man's faith. My firsthand encounter with God's faithfulness to hear our pleas began with my father and continues today as I witness it in the lives of my husband, my son, and a host of husbands whose wives call out to God in prayer.

As a wife, you have the power to open the floodgates of heaven through prayer on your husband's behalf. Whether your husband hasn't yet decided to follow Christ, has a lukewarm fledgling faith, or lives a fiery firm faith, there is no one more qualified to pray for his relationship with Christ than you. No matter where your husband is on the continuum of faithlessness to faithfulness, I encourage you to pray with "the assurance of things hoped for, the conviction of things not seen" (Hebrews 11:1, NASB).

Before we jump into praying for our husbands, let's take a look at your position as a prayer warrior, the power and purpose of intercession, and the promises of persistent prayer.

We'll begin by looking at the first married couple ever: Adam and Eve.

Then God Created an *Ezer*

"In the beginning…"

Those three little words are pregnant with anticipation, and God does not disappoint. Genesis 1:1 tells us, "In the beginning God created the heavens and the earth." God said, "Let there be," and there was. "By the word of the LORD were the heavens made, their starry host by the breath of his mouth" (Psalm 33:6). God decorated the sky with the sun, moon, and stars, separated the seas from the land, scattered seed of every kind in the soil, and released flocks of birds into the sky, swarms of insects into the air, and schools of fish into the sea. On the sixth day, God created all the creeping animals. And He wrapped up His work with a masterful flourish. "Then God said, 'Let us make man in our image, in our likeness.…' So God created man in his own image, in the image of God he created him; male and female he created them" (Genesis 1:26–27).

Then, as if the writer really wanted us to fully grasp what transpired during the first week of the earth's existence, he picked up his pen and told the story again. In Genesis 2:4, he starts over: "This is the account of the heavens and the earth when they were created."

This time when the writer got to the part about God creating man, he interjected God's musing after He formed Adam and breathed the breath of life into his lungs. God sat back, considered the lone male, and decided, "It is not good for the man to be alone" (Genesis 2:18).

This is where you come in.

"I will make a helper suitable for him," God declared. So God set out to fashion His final masterpiece. The crowning touch of His creation. Woman.

Up to this point in the creation account, we have no recorded words from Adam. However, when he laid eyes on the fair Eve, I imagine he said, "Now this is good!" His exact words were, "This is now bone of my bones and flesh of my flesh; she shall be called 'woman,' for she was taken out of man" (Genesis 2:23). Woman—the inspiration of man's first poetry and the grand finale of God's creative genius.

Let's back up, replay the scene, and take a look at one particular word God used in the creation account. God said, "I will make a *helper* suitable for him" (Genesis 2:18). The Hebrew word translated here as "helper" in reference to the woman is *ezer.* This term is derived from a Hebrew word used of God and the Holy Spirit: *azar.* Both mean "helper"—one who comes alongside to aid, assist, or rescue. The ESV Study Bible notes that the "helper" is one who supplies strength in the area that is lacking in "the helped."

Ezer appears twenty-one times in the Old Testament. Two times it is used of the woman in Genesis 2, and sixteen times it is used to describe God or Yahweh as the helper of His people. The remaining three references appear in the books of the prophets, referring to military aid. Interestingly the sixteen times the word *ezer* is used of God, it also carries military connotations. "O LORD, be my helper," David cried (Psalm 30:10, NASB). "My father's God was my helper; he saved me from the sword of Pharaoh," Moses proclaimed (Exodus 18:4). Clearly, the word *ezer* suggests a role of great honor. It is a portrait of great strength.

Theologian William Mounce painted a poignant picture:

> With so many references to God as our helper, it is obvious that an *ezer* is in no way inferior to the one who receives help. This is important because this is the word that God uses in Gen. 2:18, when he says about Adam, "It is not good for the man to be alone. I will make a *helper* suitable for him." God then forms Eve as his *ezer.* According to God's design, therefore, the man and the woman, the husband and the wife, have been designed by God to stand together and help each other fight the battles of life. And God is there as the divine *ezer* to fight with them.[1]

I was surprised to discover that even the Proverbs 31 woman, the model for godly wives and mothers through the centuries, was also referred to in military terms. "An excellent wife, who can find?" the passage begins.

"Her worth is far above jewels" (Proverbs 31:10, NASB). The New International Version calls her "a wife of noble character." The Amplified Bible describes her as "a capable, intelligent, and virtuous woman." The Hebrew word that is translated "excellent" or "virtuous" can also mean "wealthy, prosperous, valiant, boldly courageous, powerful, mighty warrior."[2] Did you catch that? *Mighty warrior.*

In my book *What God Really Thinks About Women*, I noted the following:

> God did not create woman simply because man was lonely....
> He [fashioned] woman to complete man—to love with him,
> work with him, rule with him, live life with him, procreate with
> him, and to fight alongside him. She was a female image bearer in
> this mysterious union of marriage. Woman was and is a warrior
> called to fight alongside man in the greatest battle that was yet to
> come—a battle not fought on the battlefield with guns, but on
> our knees in prayer.[3]

I'm not suggesting you replace your jeans with battle fatigues and your cute shoes with army boots. But I am suggesting that God has given you an amazing role as a prayer warrior on your husband's behalf.

The apostle Paul urges believers to enter into spiritual battle armed and ready with the Word of God.

> Finally, be strong in the Lord and in his mighty power. Put on
> the full armor of God so that you can take your stand against the
> devil's schemes. For our struggle is not against flesh and blood,
> but against the rulers, against the authorities, against the powers
> of this dark world and against the spiritual forces of evil in the
> heavenly realms. Therefore put on the full armor of God, so
> that when the day of evil comes, you may be able to stand your
> ground, and after you have done everything, to stand. Stand firm

then, with the belt of truth buckled around your waist, with the breastplate of righteousness in place, and with your feet fitted with the readiness that comes from the gospel of peace. In addition to all this, take up the shield of faith, with which you can extinguish all the flaming arrows of the evil one. Take the helmet of salvation and the sword of the Spirit, which is the word of God. And pray in the Spirit on all occasions.... Be alert and always keep on praying for all the saints. (Ephesians 6:10–18)

A spiritual battle is going on all around us, and Paul urges us to be prepared, spiritually armed and physically alert. He emphasizes this again in his second letter to the Corinthians: "Though we live in the world, we do not wage war as the world does. The weapons we fight with are not the weapons of the world. On the contrary, they have divine power to demolish strongholds" (2 Corinthians 10:3–4).

While we don't have authority over our husbands, we do have authority over the Enemy who seeks to harm him (Luke 10:19). Through prayer, the Enemy's plans are intercepted; the principalities and authorities are defeated. Through prayer, the power and provision of God flow into the lives of His people.

Paul tells us that marriage between a woman and a man is an earthly example of a heavenly relationship between Christ and the Church (Ephesians 5:22–33). So of course the devil, Satan, wants to destroy that microcosmic snapshot. He began with the first couple in the Garden of Eden, and he continues his all-out assault on the God-ordained institution of marriage today. The words of Genesis 3:1, "Now the serpent," continue to slither into marriages just as surely as they did with the first couple of all time.

But here's the good news. Jesus said, "But take heart! I have overcome the world" (John 16:33). Not only that, Jesus said He has given you power and authority to "overcome all the power of the enemy" (Luke 10:19). "The one who is in you is greater than the one who is in the world"

(1 John 4:4). You are an *ezer*, uniquely fashioned and supernaturally equipped to do battle on your knees in prayer for your marriage and your man.

The Purpose of Prayer

"Well, I guess the only thing left to do is pray about it." How many times have I heard those words? How many times have they slipped past my lips? But what if we looked at prayer from a different perspective...God's perspective? What if we viewed prayer as our first course of action rather than a last resort?

The vast majority of the e-mails I receive through my ministry center on marriage problems. Women struggle with husbands who aren't living up to their expectations: men who work too much and love too little, men who withdraw emotionally and advance sexually, men who initially appear to be Prince Charming but later reveal the villain within.

Some wives describe their husbands as hardhearted, meanspirited, and verbally combative. Others complain that their husbands are aloof, passive, and emotionally withdrawn. Perhaps your man fits one of those descriptions.

On the other hand, perhaps you have an adoring husband who cherishes you, cares for you, and encourages you to be all that God has created you to be. Praise God for such a man!

Regardless of where your man or your marriage falls on the continuum of terrific to tolerable to terrible, there is always room for improvement. Prayer can make a bad marriage good and a good marriage great.

Before we start, I want to make this very clear: Prayer is not a means of *gaining control* over your husband, to whip him into shape and make him the man *you* want him to be. Prayer is a means of *relinquishing control* of your husband and asking God to shape him into the man that *He* wants him to be. Prayer involves turning the finger that points out your man's faults and folding it along with the others in prayer.

The Bible tells us in Isaiah 29:16, "You turn things upside down, as if the potter were thought to be like the clay! Shall what is formed say to him who formed it, 'He did not make me'? Can the pot say of the potter, 'He knows nothing'?"

God is the Master Potter, and He certainly doesn't need you or me to tell Him how to shape and mold that marvelous piece of pottery called husband. Oh, we'd like to. That's for sure. But God's ultimate goal is for that lump of clay to be fashioned according to His design and for His purposes, not ours. "We are the clay, you are the potter," Isaiah writes, "we are all the work of your hand" (Isaiah 64:8). I am. You are. Your husband is.

God shapes and molds. You pray and intercede. James warns about the danger of praying with wrong motives (James 4:3). Check your desire to control at the door of the prayer closet and don't let it in.

Prayer is not for the purpose of getting your husband to do what you want him to do when you want him to do it. Let me take that a bit further. Prayer is not for the purpose of getting God to do what you want Him to do when you want Him to do it. It is not for twisting God's arm to convince Him to do your bidding. He already has your best interests in mind. He already has your husband's best interests in mind. Amazingly, He invites you to play a part in the miracle of making your husband into the man He created him to be. Your role is not to nag, manipulate, cajole, or control. Your part is to love him and pray for him. And as you pray, God aligns your desires with His desires, your thinking with His thinking, and your heart with His heart.

God is not hoarding His blessings, waiting for us to say the right words to pry those blessings out of His stingy hand. He longs to lavish us with His goodness! (Ephesians 1:7–8). And yet He often waits for us to ask. I am not saying I understand it. Prayer is simply how He chose to engineer the flow of His power and activity from the spiritual realm into the physical realm. Prayer is the conduit through which God's power is released and His will is brought to earth as it is in heaven.

It is not that God cannot act without the prayers of His people. He can do anything He pleases (Psalm 115:3). However, He has established prayer as the gate through which His blessings flow. James reminds us: "You do not have, because you do not ask" (James 4:2).

Ezekiel gives us a glimpse into the heart of God regarding prayer. Israel had sinned in every possible way, and her people were doomed for destruction. God said, "I looked for a man among them who would build up the wall and stand before me in the gap on behalf of the land so I would not have to destroy it, but I found none" (Ezekiel 22:30). God looked for someone to pray, to intercede, to stand in the gap for Israel, but there was no one.

Today God is looking for women who will stand in the gap for their husbands, wives who will pray for their men to experience the fullness of God's blessing. I'm so glad He has found such a woman in you.

The Power of Persistent Prayer

Since that day in the bride room, I have spent many hours praying for my husband. I don't have a big bad story of how God took our terrible tumultuous marriage and miraculously transformed it into a storybook romance filled with white knight rescues, relentless romance, and rides into the sunset as we left all danger and darkness behind. Even though we've had our share of both tumult and romance, our relationship is no fairy tale. Our marriage reads more like a daily journal, one page after another, one day after another. Eleven thousand, six hundred, and eighty at the time of this writing. Some entries are smudged with tears; others are dog-eared as favorites. Some pages of our story are marred by unsuccessful erasures that wouldn't quite rub away the words said; others are finger-worn by reading of precious events time and time again.

For most couples, life is just daily. However, the accumulation of small struggles can nibble like termites to undermine the foundation of what appears to be a healthy structure just as surely as an earthshaking rumble of sudden disaster.

In our early years of marriage, my prayers for Steve were more conflict oriented. I tended to pray for him when I felt he "needed" it. When a difficult situation arose, when work was hard, when finances were strained, when relationships were messy, when stress had us both tightly wound. And yes, I did see God's hand respond to those prayers of intercession on my husband's behalf. But as my understanding of prayer matured, so did my intercession for Steve. My desperate cries to God in difficulties grew into daily conversations with God in the ordinary. I prayed for God's protection and provision for my man in the one-step-in-front-of-the-other dailiness of life.

And while my marriage has not miraculously come back from the brink of disaster, I have held the hands of women who have experienced exactly that. Beth, whose husband was addicted to pornography, but because of her intercession sought out help and deliverance. Jona, whose husband filed for divorce, but because of her intercession fell in love with her all over again. Patty, whose husband was consumed with work and financial gain, but because of her intercession turned his heart back toward home. Miriam, whose husband was bound by pain from past abuse, but because of her intercession experienced the freedom of healing and forgiveness. I have held their hands. I have heard their cries. I have joined in their prayers. I have witnessed their miracles.

You may be wondering if your marriage is too far gone. Too much pain to patch. Too much hurt to heal. Too many mistakes to mend. Too much resentment to remedy. Too much bitterness to make better. Too much brokenness to rebuild. Too much betrayal to forgive. Too much. Too much. Too much.

I realize that you might have picked this book up as a last resort. Perhaps you feel your marriage is in such a shambles, there is absolutely nothing you can do *but* pray. Well, praise God for that! I'm glad you haven't given up. God's specialty is resurrection. He brings the dead to life...and that includes marriages that seem beyond hope.

The Bible shows us time and time again that what is impossible for man is possible with God. When God told Abraham that his eighty-nine-year-old wife was going to have a son, the eavesdropping Sarah laughed. God's messenger calmly replied, "Is anything too hard for the LORD?" (Genesis 18:14).

In the New Testament, we find similar words when the angel Gabriel appeared to a young virgin girl named Mary and told her she was going to conceive a son. "'How will this be,' Mary asked the angel, 'since I am a virgin?'" Gabriel replied, "Nothing is impossible with God" (Luke 1:26–38).

Not convinced? Let me give you one more example. Let's go back to the Old Testament to a prophet named Ezekiel. One day God brought Ezekiel to the middle of a large valley. It wasn't a lush landscape filled with beautiful foliage but rather a wasteland littered with human bones. These weren't just any ol' bones. The prophet describes them as "bones that were very dry" (Ezekiel 37:2). In other words, these bones had been dead a long time. Bones, bones, everywhere bones. Ezekiel describes what happened to these long-dead, dry bones:

> Then he [God] said to me, "Prophesy to these bones and say to them, 'Dry bones, hear the word of the LORD! This is what the Sovereign LORD says to these bones: I will make breath enter you, and you will come to life. I will attach tendons to you and make flesh come upon you and cover you with skin; I will put breath in you, and you will come to life. Then you will know that I am the LORD.'"
>
> So I prophesied as I was commanded. And as I was prophesying, there was a noise, a rattling sound, and the bones came together, bone to bone. I looked, and tendons and flesh appeared on them and skin covered them, but there was no breath in them.
>
> Then he said to me, "Prophesy to the breath; prophesy, son of man, and say to it, 'This is what the Sovereign LORD says: Come from the four winds, O breath, and breathe into these slain, that they may live.'" So I prophesied as he commanded me,

and breath entered them; they came to life and stood up on their feet—a vast army. (37:4–10)

Now that would have been a sight to behold. Oh friend, you may feel that your marriage resembles that valley of dry bones. Not just any ol' bones, but long-dead, dry bones. It may seem that your marriage has passed the point of no return. But our God specializes in bringing death to life. He can turn a valley of bones into a vast army, and He can transform a marriage of pain into a living, breathing, walking testimony of mercy and grace.

For nothing is impossible with God.

How thankful I am that He has invited me and you to join Him in His work—to participate in the miraculous through powerful intercession.

How to Use This Book

I find that many women, including me, are directionally challenged. I need landmarks. Don't tell me to go east or west, north or south. Give me a landmark. Turn right at the McDonald's. Turn left at the fire station. Look for the teal-colored house around the bend. Those are directions that I can follow.

Maybe that's why I love the fact that Jesus taught His disciples to pray using landmarks. When one of His disciples asked, "Lord, teach us to pray" (Luke 11:1), Jesus responded:

In this manner, therefore, pray:
Our Father in heaven,
Hallowed be Your name.
Your kingdom come.
Your will be done
On earth as it is in heaven.
Give us this day our daily bread.

And forgive us our debts,
As we forgive our debtors.
And do not lead us into temptation,
But deliver us from the evil one.
For Yours is the kingdom and the power
      and the glory forever. Amen.
      (Matthew 6:9–13, NKJV)

Jesus was not instructing the disciples on how to pray a rote prayer. He was giving them a *pattern* for prayer—landmarks: Acknowledge God's fatherhood, holiness, and sovereignty. Ask for His will to be done, your needs to be met, and your sins to be forgiven. Ask for deliverance from temptation and protection from evil. Acknowledge God's rule, reign, power, and glory.

In a similar way, *Praying for Your Husband from Head to Toe* will give you landmarks to guide your prayers. This is not a magic formula or a pattern for rote prayer. It is simply a guide for pursuing a more consistent and effective prayer life.

Let's be honest. God's ways are not our ways, and sometimes we don't know what to pray for our husbands. But we can rest assured that when we pray the *Word of God,* we pray the *will of God.* What a relief!

When Paul instructed us to put on the armor of God, did you notice there was only one weapon? Everything else—the figurative helmet, breastplate, belt, shield, and shoes—were defensive pieces intended for protection from the Evil One. The sword of the Spirit, which is defined as the Word of God, is the only offensive weapon listed in the whole outfit.

After Paul instructed us to take up the sword of the Spirit, he followed with this: "And pray in the Spirit on all occasions" (Ephesians 6:18). When you combine the Word of God with Spirit-empowered prayer, you are armed and dangerous against the power of the Enemy. You have "divine power to demolish strongholds" (2 Corinthians 10:4).

In the Greek, the original language of the New Testament, the word translated as "power" is *dunamis;* it speaks of "potential power" and "actual power." It is where we get our English word *dynamite.* God has handed you two powerful sticks of "dynamite" as you intercede for your husband: His Word and prayer. As you strap these two sticks together and ignite the fuse with faith, you will see the power of God act on your and your husband's behalf as never before.

In the next section I will provide an overview of the landmarks we'll be using to pray for our husbands. Each landmark is represented by a part of your husband's body; for example, his mind represents what he thinks about; his eyes, what he looks at; his ears, what he listens to; and so on. This will be your road map as you cover your man in prayer.

In part 2 we begin to pray. I have provided a thirty-day guide for interceding for your husband from head to toe. Each day you'll find a scripture for each landmark and a prayer that incorporates that passage. It should take approximately five to seven minutes to cover your husband daily in powerfully effective, Bible-based prayer. I can't think of a better investment of time!

Throughout this book, the prayers are written as if your husband were a Christian. However, I recognize there is no greater burden for a woman than for her unsaved husband and children to come to know Jesus as Savior and Lord. All else pales in the light of where they will spend eternity. If your husband has not yet made a decision to follow Christ, you'll find scriptures in the appendix that target that most important need of all. As we go through the thirty days of prayer, we will be praying by faith, calling "things that are not as though they were" (Romans 4:17).

One way to use the book is to correspond the days of prayer with the dates of the months. For example, on the first day of the month, pray day one; on the second day of the month, pray day two; and so on. If you miss a day, just stay on track with your calendar, then begin again the following month. Of course you can also simply pray straight through without connecting the days of prayer with the dates on the calendar.

If you're like me, you will want to use this book time and time again. You might even want to gather a few girlfriends to form a Praying Wives group and pray for your husbands together. Jesus said, "Again, I tell you that if two of you on earth *agree* about anything you ask for, it will be done for you by my Father in heaven" (Matthew 18:19). The Greek word for "agree" is *symphōneō,* which means "to sound together, to be in accord, primarily of musical instruments."[4] What a beautiful symphony wafts to the heavenlies when sisters in Christ join in harmonious prayer offered up to God!

Just make sure the group sticks to praying and not complaining. You don't want that beautiful symphony to sound like the cat-scratching tuning of the instruments before the actual symphony begins.

No matter which way you choose to use this prayer guide, I know you and your husband will be blessed "exceedingly abundantly" above all you ask or think! (Ephesians 3:20, NKJV).

I have set up a web page to help us pray for one another's husbands. You can log on to www.prayingforyourhusband.com to share your prayer requests and to pray for others. You can also share your victories, and we will celebrate with you!

Before you begin, let me give you a little warning. There will be days when you will not want to pray for your husband—days when you don't feel like asking God to bless him. There will be times when what you really want to do is ask God to knock him upside the head because he's hurt your feelings, been mean to you, or disappointed you. But let me encourage you to pray anyway. I can't tell you how many times I've been upset with Steve and then as I prayed *for* him, God softened my heart *toward* him. And pray for yourself too. Pray that God will give you a forgiving heart, a grace-filled attitude, and a sacrificial love.

Praying for your husband will do more than impact your husband's life; it will impact your heart as well. Don't be surprised if God stirs a love for your husband that is stronger, deeper, and more precious than ever before. As I wrote this book and spent many hours praying for Steve, God did a work in my heart I wasn't expecting.

I'm so excited to see how God is going to act on your behalf as you lift up your man in prayer. The prophet Isaiah wrote this about God: "Since ancient times no one has heard, no ear has perceived, no eye has seen any God besides you, who acts on behalf of those who wait for him" (Isaiah 64:4).

Now let's look at the road map and the landmarks for this guide on how to pray for your husband from head to toe.

The Landmarks of Prayer: From Head to Toe

The complexities of the human body reflect the inexplicable wisdom and unfathomable power of our infinitely creative God. Contemplating the sheer beauty of how man and woman fit perfectly together as two pieces of a magnificently crafted puzzle makes my heart quicken. As we embark on this journey of praying for our husbands from head to toe, we will use physical landmarks of his outer body to represent spiritual, psychological, and emotional aspects of his inner man. So let's get started praying for that fabulous work of art—your husband.

His Mind: *What He Thinks About*

Let's start with a little anatomy lesson.

When God created man and woman in His own image, He created each human as a triune being with a body, soul, and spirit. The earthly body is the part we see, and it houses our five senses: smell, touch, taste, sight, and hearing. The body is a temporary "earth suit" that will one day pass away and return to dust. Paul refers to the body as a "tent" (2 Corinthians 5:1, 4). For those who join Jesus in heaven, it will be replaced with a heavenly body. That's exciting news!

The spirit is the inner man that communicates with God and lives for eternity. This is the part that is "born again" when someone comes to Christ. The Bible tells us that after Adam and Eve sinned, everyone is born with a dead spirit (Romans 5:12). However, the moment someone believes in Jesus as Savior and Lord, his or her dead spirit comes to life and lives for all eternity with God (Ephesians 2:1–5). That is even more exciting news!

The third part of man, the soul, is what makes up the personality. Both the spirit and the soul are immaterial or invisible but very distinct. The writer of Hebrews tells us: "For the word of God is living and active. Sharper than any double-edged sword, it penetrates even to dividing *soul and spirit*, joints and marrow" (Hebrews 4:12). Paul encouraged the Thessalonians: "May your whole spirit, soul and body be kept blameless at the coming of our Lord Jesus Christ" (1 Thessalonians 5:23).

The soul includes the mind, will, and emotions. We receive information into our minds, we act on that information with our wills, and we feel a response with our emotions. The brain is part of the body and is different from the mind. The mind actually uses the brain just as we use a computer to store, enter, process, and search for information.

With that brief spiritual anatomy lesson, you can see why we're starting at the top by praying for your husband's mind. So many times we try to change the way we act. However, we cannot consistently act differently than we think or believe. That is why Scripture tells us, "Do not be conformed to this world, but be transformed by the renewing of your *mind*" (Romans 12:2, NASB). Godly thinking produces godly actions. The writer of Proverbs says it this way: "For as he [man] thinks within himself, so he is" (Proverbs 23:7, NASB).

Throughout the prayers I will use the word *flesh*. In the Bible, this word can mean the physical body, but it can also mean the old thought processes and habit patterns we develop apart from Christ. Let me give you a definition of *flesh* that I want you to keep in mind as you pray: *flesh* is the way we program our minds and actions to get our God-given needs met apart from Christ. As soon as we are born, we begin developing thoughts and habit patterns to get our needs met. As soon as we are *born again* through a relationship with Christ, we must begin renewing our minds with the truth of God's Word to transform those old ways of thinking and acting to conform to the image of Christ. The goal is to stop living according to the flesh (our old ways of getting our needs met apart from

Christ) and start living according to the Spirit (allowing the Holy Spirit to control our thoughts and actions).

As you pray for your husband's mind, you'll be praying for the thoughts that come into his mind, tumble about in his head, and affect his actions and emotions. You'll be praying for God to guard his thought life, to keep ungodly thoughts out and wholesome thoughts in.

His Eyes: *What He Looks At*

When God created Adam, and every man thereafter, He fashioned them to be visual creatures. All men are highly influenced by what they see, and what they look at affects what they think about.

If you want to get an idea of what tempts your husband's eyes, take some time to watch commercials during sporting events. Advertisers have spent billions of dollars to discover what lures a man's eyes to trigger a desired response, images that hit the bull's-eye of a man's weak spot to cause him to make a purchase. Advertisers push the idea that he would be envied if he drove their model car, he would be successful if he wore their brand of clothes, he would be manly if he used their specific razor, he would be sexy if he wore their enticing cologne, he would have friends if he drank their special brew, he would be happy if he ate their savory snack, he would be athletic if he wore their performance shoes.

Visual lassos can capture a man's soul and tie him in knots of dissatisfaction and discontentment. A clear example of the magnetic pull of advertising to create a sense of dissatisfaction was seen in an American company that opened a new plant in Central America because the labor was plentiful and inexpensive.

Everything went well until the villagers received their first paycheck; afterward they did not return to work. Several days later, the manager went down to the village chief to determine the cause of this problem, and the chief responded, "Why should we work? We already have everything we need." The plant stood idle for two months until someone came up with the idea of sending a mail-order catalog to every villager. There has never been an employment problem since.[5]

Advertisers are quick to say, "Sex sells." Throw a seductive woman into any commercial, and it captures a man's attention like nothing else. We live in a sex-saturated culture filled with visual land mines ready to explode and destroy a man's thought life. An enticing billboard. A seductive window display at the mall. A lingerie advertisement in the newspaper. The onslaught of suggestive images hits a man at every turn. While your husband can't avoid the sexual images that bombard him throughout the day, he can choose to look away and take every thought captive.

Please don't get mad because your husband is hard-wired to look where he should not look. Rather, pray that he can overcome the temptation and turn his eyes away. Both happily married men who love their wives and miserable men who are longing for a way out have difficulty keeping their eyes focused in a godly direction.

You are not called to police your husband's actions but to pray. Don't spend your time fighting against your man by pointing out every time he looks at something he shouldn't. Instead, invest your time praying for him to have the willpower not to look at what he shouldn't and the desire to keep his focus on what he should.

As you pray for your husband's eyes, you'll be praying for the windows to his soul to be open wide to all God has to bless him, while the blinds remain closed to anything the Enemy would use to distract or destroy him.

His Ears: *What He Listens To*

All day long your husband is assailed by noise. It begins with the buzz of the alarm clock and ends with the click of the bedside lamp. In between the bookends of his day, his ears are barraged with ringing cell phones, roaring cars, honking horns, piercing sirens, demanding bosses, questioning employees, chatty coworkers, blaring televisions, singing radios, buzzing pagers, inquisitive children, and a talkative wife (at least that's true at my house).

And just as with what he looks at, what he listens to affects his thoughts, actions, and emotions. While your husband cannot turn off the world's noise, you can pray he will tune in to what is helpful and tune out what is harmful. You can pray that he will raise his spiritual antennae to detect the frequency of God's voice in his inner man.

All through the Bible we read of God speaking to men and women right in the middle of the hustle and bustle of their busy days. He spoke to Moses while he was tending sheep (Exodus 3), to Gideon while he was threshing wheat (Judges 6), to shepherds while they were watching flocks (Luke 2), to Peter, James, and John while they were casting nets (Luke 5), and to Levi (Matthew) while he was collecting taxes (Luke 5). God even spoke to Peter while he was taking a nap (Acts 11). And He can speak to your husband right smack-dab in the middle of his busy day as well.

Hearing God's voice is not only for the "super Christian," if there is such a thing. It is for the uneducated fisherman (Matthew 4:21), the common shepherd (Exodus 3), the book-smart school teacher (John 3:1–21), the stodgy government official (John 18:18–24), the less-than-honest tax collector (Luke 19:1–9), the hardened soldier (Luke 22:50–53), the hardworking farmer (Judges 6), the condemned criminal (Luke 23:39–43), and the husband going out the door to face the daily grind. You can pray your husband will be sensitive to God's gentle whisper in his noisy day.

As you pray for your husband's ears, you'll be praying for what he listens to—that he will tune in to what is helpful and tune out what is harmful.

His Mouth: *The Words He Speaks*

When God created the world, He did so with words. He spoke, and what was not became what is. "By the word of the LORD were the heavens made, their starry host by the breath of his mouth" (Psalm 33:6). God said, "Let there be," and then there was. Amazingly, when He created mankind in His own image, He gave us the incredible gift of words. Creative. Powerful. Words.

The Bible tells us, "Death and life are in the power of the tongue" (Proverbs 18:21, NASB). God told the Israelites, "I will do to you the very things I heard you *say*" (Numbers 14:28). Jesus said to speak to a mountain and it would be removed (Mark 11:23). Many great miracles in the Bible occurred because someone spoke. Jesus healed the sick, cast out demons, raised the dead, calmed the storm, and withered a fig tree…with only the power of His words.

Your husband's life is a canvas, and his words are the brush that creates a portrait of glory and grace…or at least they could be. With the words he speaks, he shapes the world around him, either building others up or tearing them down. Our words become the mirrors in which others see themselves, and your husband's words affect the lives of people he comes in contact with throughout the day. Like a rudder on a ship or a bridle in a horse's mouth, your husband's words will determine the course of his very life (James 3:3–6).

There's good news and bad news when it comes to taming the tongue. James tells us the bad news: "All kinds of animals, birds, reptiles and creatures of the sea are being tamed and have been tamed by man, but no man can tame the tongue" (James 3:7–8). But Gabriel tells us the good news: "Nothing is impossible with God" (Luke 1:37). What a relief!

As you pray for your husband's mouth, you'll be praying that the words he speaks will have a positive impact in his life and in the lives of the people in his sphere of influence. You'll be praying that God will set a guard over his mouth and keep watch over the door of his lips (Psalm 141:3).

His Neck: *The Decisions That Turn His Head*

Perhaps you've seen the movie *My Big Fat Greek Wedding*—one of my favorites. The main character, Toula Portokalos, is a thirty-year-old single Greek woman who works in her family's restaurant, Dancing Zorba's. Her father, Gus, wants her to marry a nice Greek boy and have nice Greek children. But Toula wants more out of life. She gets a job at her aunt's travel agency and meets Ian Miller, a high school English teacher. Ian is a nice boy, but he is not a Greek boy. When Toula's father discovers his daughter is dating a non-Greek, he demands their relationship come to a halt.

Toula and Ian want to get married, but she knows her father would never approve. Her mother is sympathetic to her daughter's dilemma and agrees to help.

"Ma, Dad is so stubborn. What he says goes," Toula cries. "Ah, the man is the head of the house!"

"Let me tell you something, Toula," her mother assures her. "The man is the head, but the woman is the neck. And she can turn the head any way she wants."

That scene prompts laughter every time. We all know exactly what Mrs. Portokalos meant.

But in real life, a wife's attempts at manipulation are no laughing matter. Here's another idea. Rather than a wife being the neck that turns her husband's head, slyly manipulating him into making decisions that suit her fancy, what if she stepped aside and let God be the One turning his head?

We've looked at various features of your husband's head: his mind, his eyes, his ears, and his mouth. And now we get to that vertical connection. As Mrs. Portokalos so aptly described, the neck is what turns the head.

Today's world teems with choices. Wheel a cart down the aisle of any grocery store and you'll find a microcosm of our choice-saturated culture. With 48,750 items on the average supermarket shelves, including 91 different shampoos, 93 varieties of toothpaste, and 115 types of household cleaners,[6] a quick trip to the grocery store becomes a stressful decision-making event. Even Starbucks, where we go to take a break from the hustle and bustle (or get fueled up to face it), offers consumers up to 87,000 possible drink combinations.[7]

Beyond the choices of what to buy and when to buy it, a man's head can be set spinning by the choices of how to live life. To have children now or wait. To stay at the job or find a new one. To relocate for a better economic climate or stay put. To buy or rent. To invest or save. To toss a ball with his son or stay an extra two hours at the office. To engage with his wife or pick up the remote. Options, while they seem like a positive ideal on the surface, can become the quicksand that bogs us down. Rather than liberate, the overbearing pressure of choices can actually debilitate. In fact, research "shows that an excess of choices often leads us to be less, not more, satisfied once we actually decide. There's often that nagging feeling we could have done better."[8]

Choice. It was God's gift to mankind in the Garden of Eden. What will your man do with that gift? Will Jesus be the North Star of his moral compass? Or will he be swayed by the ever-changing mores of a culture that takes what is wrong today and, with the vote of a majority, makes it right tomorrow? Will he choose to make honoring God his highest priority or default to pleasing self?

As you pray for your husband's neck, you'll be praying for the choices he makes throughout the day, asking God to turn his head *toward* the abundant life Jesus came to give and *away from* the self-centered life that can never satisfy.

His Shoulders: *His Burdens and Worries*

"I feel like I have the weight of the whole world on my shoulders," Bob moans. And we know exactly what he means. Burdens prey on a man's soul as he considers the future and feels responsible for the outcome. Responsible for his family's safety. Responsible for his family's finances. Responsible for his health. Responsible for his wife's happiness. Responsible for his children's future. Responsible for his company's success.

And all that responsibility heaped up high often brings worry, anxiety, and tangled emotions. Bundles of burdens piled on a man's shoulders are tied taut with the ropes of "what if." *What if the economy doesn't turn around and we lose our savings? What if I can't be a good father? What if I can't please my wife? What if my business fails? What if I lose my job? What if...*

There is a difference between a healthy sense of responsibility and the unhealthy weight of burdens. I am not advocating the "Don't worry, be happy" mantra of the lazy and irresponsible. I'm not suggesting the "whatever" attitude of the reckless and lackadaisical. The Bible says to work hard, do your part, and avoid laziness (Proverbs 14:23). But it also says not to worry about the outcome. Don't be anxious about what tomorrow brings (Philippians 4:6). God is in control.

The fact is, there would be plenty to worry about if the outcome of our lives depended on human effort alone. But it doesn't. When a husband understands that God invites him to cast all his burdens on God's shoulders (Psalm 55:22), he is freed to do his best and leave the outcome to God.

In times past men carried heavy loads on their shoulders. In some parts of the world, they still do. And while you may not be able to see the burdens strapped on your man's shoulders, they are there. So that's going to be our focus for this landmark of prayer.

As you pray for your husband's shoulders, you'll be lifting up his worries and burdens to the only One able to carry them all.

His Heart: *Who or What He Loves*

"There she blows!" I yelled as the geyser shot up in the air. I knew it was corny and that thousands had shouted the same silly words before, but I just couldn't help myself.

My family and I had waited for over an hour in July heat for Old Faithful in Yellowstone National Park to perform her magic. Right on cue, she shot 8,400 gallons of boiling water 150 feet into the air to the delight of a cheering crowd. The show lasted about three minutes and promised a repeat performance every seventy-six minutes or so.

We hung around just to see if she would do it again. She did. The seemingly endless supply of water below the surface of the earth, combined with heat and pressure, performs a watery spectacle that faithfully does not disappoint.

After making sure we had covered all the photo ops for posterity, we hopped in the car to see the next natural wonder at Yellowstone: the Sulfur Caldron, a series of stinky-smelling sulfurous ponds that bubble up from below the earth's surface. These putrid puddles may have been a geothermal marvel, but we didn't see many tourists hanging around to gaze at their beauty. The stench was horrific. I clicked a few pictures, and then we made a quick getaway—with the car windows shut tight.

Driving away, I pondered the two watery world wonders. One was fresh, clean, beautiful, resplendent, faithful. The other was foul, repugnant, vile, smelly, stagnant. Both were watery displays, but with very different results…much like the human heart.

The Bible refers to the heart as the "wellspring of life" (Proverbs 4:23). Everything we do flows from it. The heart is the hidden spring of life that directs the course of our daily choices and lifelong decisions. In the Bible, the heart is the seat of joy (John 16:22), desires (Matthew 5:28), affections (Luke 24:32), perceptions (John 12:40), thoughts (Matthew 9:4), understanding (Matthew 13:15), reasoning (Mark 2:6), imagination (Luke 1:51), conscience (Acts 2:37), intentions (Hebrews 4:12), purpose (Acts 11:23), will (Romans 6:17), and faith (Mark 11:23).[9]

Your husband's heart is the hub of the wheel into which all the spokes of his life are attached. When a man's heart is right with God, everything else falls into place. In the words of my country grandmother, "What is down in the well will come up in the bucket."

As you pray for your husband's heart, you'll be praying for what and who he loves, the priorities and the people he treasures. You'll be praying for the wellspring from which all of his life flows.

His Back: *His Protection*

It was a beautiful, crisp February morning when Steve and I traveled from the University of North Carolina at Chapel Hill to his family's home in Charlotte to announce our engagement. The night before, God had decorated His creation with a dusting of snow and tipped the trees with shimmering icicles. All of nature looked as if it were dressed for a wedding.

After the grand announcement and a warm meal, we headed back to school. The day had warmed and melted most of the snow, but nightfall brought freezing temperatures and slick roads. As we neared our college town, we began descending the crest of a hill and struck a patch of ice. The tires hit the slick surface, and the car spun out of control.

"Steve! We're headed straight for that car," I cried as a set of oncoming headlights shone through the windshield.

Seeing there was nothing he could do, Steve took his hands off the steering wheel and cried out, "Oh, God! Save us!"

One second we were headed directly toward an oncoming car. The next we were sitting off the side of the road in a ditch, facing the opposite direction with our bodies pinned safely back against our seats. This was before seat belt laws, and we were not buckled up.

"How did we miss that car?" I asked. "Where did it go?"

Shaken, Steve replied, "There's only one answer to those questions: God."

God is our Protector—our Stronghold in times of trouble (Psalm 18:2), our Shield in times of danger (Proverbs 30:5), and our Fortress in times of attack (Psalm 91:1–2). Not only that, God promises to "command his angels concerning you to guard you in all your ways" (Psalm 91:11).

God protects us not only in the physical realm that we can see but also in the spiritual realm against forces we can't see (2 Corinthians 10:3–4). A spiritual battle rages around your husband as the devil attempts to kill, steal, and destroy (John 10:10). He sets traps in the path of God's people in hopes of catching them unaware and ill prepared.

As I mentioned earlier, Paul's letter to the Ephesians instructs us to "put on the full armor of God" (Ephesians 6:11). But his detailed description of the spiritual armor does not point to any item protecting the back. I like to think of it like this: God's got your back.

All through the Bible we read of God protecting His people. He parted rivers, calmed the seas, shut the mouths of lions, fireproofed men in a furnace, confused an army, de-venomized a snake, and rattled jail cell doors to fly open and set the disciples free. He protected Noah in a boat, Moses in a basket, and Paul in a ship. He reduced Goliath to a blustering bully, Jericho's wall to a pile of rubble, and the Egyptian pharaoh to a powerless pawn. He raised up a shepherd boy to be a king, a donkey to be a messenger, and a baby born in Bethlehem to be the Savior of the world. Oh yes, sister, God's got your back! And He's got your husband's back too.

As you pray for your husband's back, you'll be praying for his protection in the physical and spiritual realms with the assurance that no weapon formed against him will succeed (Isaiah 54:17).

His Arms: *His Strength*

The bulked-up powerlifter steps onto the competition stage with muscles bulging. He squats, wraps his fingers around the metal bar, and lifts. Off the floor. To the waist. To the chest. And finally past his grimacing face into the air. And the crowd agrees, "Wow, he's strong."

How do *you* determine how strong someone is? Many would say it is by how much weight a person can lift. Some would argue it is how much weight a body can carry. Others would say strength is determined by how long someone can endure or sustain an action. Webster's defines *strength* as "the capacity to exert force, resist attack, or resist strain, stress, etc."

In the Bible, God's strength is symbolized by His arm. The psalmist wrote: "The strong right arm of the LORD is raised in triumph. The strong right arm of the LORD has done glorious things!" (Psalm 118:16, NLT). "Powerful is your arm!" (Psalm 89:13, NLT). Moses reminded the Israelites: "Remember that you were slaves in Egypt and that the LORD your God brought you out of there with a mighty hand and an out-stretched arm" (Deuteronomy 5:15). The Israelites praised God "who sent his glorious arm of power to be at Moses' right hand" (Isaiah 63:12).

In contrast to our infinitely powerful God, all men at one time or another will struggle with feelings of weakness. Even Paul, one of the most spiritually strong men in the New Testament, grappled with feelings of inferiority, insecurity, and inadequacy. He admitted that he had "conflicts on the outside, fears within" (2 Corinthians 7:5). But God reminded him, "My grace is sufficient for you, for my power is made perfect in weakness" (2 Corinthians 12:9). I love how the Amplified Bible expounds on it:

> But He said to me, My grace (My favor and loving-kindness and mercy) is enough for you [sufficient against any danger and enables you to bear the trouble manfully]; for My strength and power are made perfect (fulfilled and completed) and show themselves most effective in [your] weakness. Therefore, I will all the more gladly glory in my weaknesses and infirmities, that the strength and power of Christ (the Messiah) may rest (yes, may pitch a tent over and dwell) upon me!

Paul tells us the secret to his success: "For when I am weak, then I am strong" (2 Corinthians 12:10) and "I can do everything through him who gives me strength" (Philippians 4:13). Human weakness becomes the backdrop for God's strength to shine.

As we come to the next landmark of prayer, your husband's arms, we'll borrow from biblical symbolism and pray for his strength. But it's not heavy lifting that will make your man spiritually and emotionally strong. True strength comes when he allows his life to become a conduit through which God's strength flows.

As you pray for your husband's arms, you'll be praying that he will not depend on his own strength but instead rely on God's strength to work in him and through him. You'll be praying for strength of character, courage, and purpose to be all God has fashioned him to be.

His Hands: *His Work*

I'll be the first to admit I don't know much about sports, but chances are your man does. I think most little boys, at some time in their lives, dream about being professional athletes. Shooting the winning basket as the crowd goes wild. Scoring the winning touchdown as the referee raises his arms. Hitting the home run with the bases loaded. And the ultimate dream would be getting paid to do it.

The truth is, only a small percentage of men actually play professional sports. However, every man desires to be the best at what he does. Whether on the construction site, in the operating room, or on a sales call, a man longs for the work of his hands to be successful, meaningful, and productive. He longs to have purpose and to leave his mark on the world that says, "I was here. I made a difference."

Right from the start, God gave Adam a job to do and a purpose to fulfill. "Fill the earth and subdue it. Rule over the fish of the sea and the birds of the air and over every living creature that moves on the ground" (Genesis 1:28). After Adam and Eve disobeyed God, their work became difficult. And even though there are thorns and thistles in every job, man is still called to work.

Some may disagree, but I believe a man's work is a source of fulfillment and purpose in a much different way than for a woman. Many times a husband measures his manhood by his ability to succeed in the workplace and provide for his family. When a man is fired, laid off, or downsized, he begins to question his value and his purpose.

Even so, work is not meant to become an idol or a measuring stick of a man's significance. We've all seen men who work too little and men who work too much. Both ends of the spectrum, laziness and workaholism, are detrimental to the God-glorifying life. About the lazy man, the Bible says: "Despite their desires, the lazy will come to ruin, for their hands refuse to work" (Proverbs 21:25, NLT). About the man who works too much, the Bible says: "Do not wear yourself out to get rich; have the wisdom to show restraint. Cast but a glance at riches, and they are gone, for they will surely sprout wings and fly off to the sky like an eagle" (Proverbs 23:4–5).

The New International Version of the Bible calls a lazy man a "sluggard" (Proverbs 6:6, 9). Webster's defines a sluggard as a "slow, inactive person." But the biblical meaning is more than simply slow. It implies a refusal to work or an avoidance of work. At the opposite end of the continuum is workaholism. Webster's defines a workaholic as one who is "addicted to work." It is one who places work above everything and everyone else in his life. A workaholic craves success, power, and financial gain to the degree that it consumes his very life.

Neither avoidance of work nor an obsession with success will bring happiness in the long run. It is the man who finds a healthy balance between the two who truly enjoys life.

One of the best ways to achieve that balance and find fulfillment in any job is wrapped up in seven little words: "Do all to the glory of God" (1 Corinthians 10:31, NASB). "All" includes hammering the nail to the glory of God. Making the sales call to the glory of God. Operating on the patient to the glory of God. Driving the delivery truck to the glory of God. Running the multimillion-dollar corporation to the glory of God. Landscaping the grounds to the glory of God.

As you pray for your husband's hands, you'll be praying for his work—that he will have a clear sense of purpose, a strong grasp of his gifting, and a deep desire to glorify God. You'll be praying he will have a positive influence and make a lasting impact on his world.

His Ring Finger: *His Marriage*
Here we are at the landmark that started all this praying in the first place: your marriage. One of God's best ideas! C. S. Lewis painted a beautiful picture of the unity of marriage in his book *Mere Christianity:*

> The Christian idea of marriage is based on Christ's words that a
> man and wife are to be regarded as a single organism—for that is
> what the words "one flesh" would be in modern English. And
> the Christians believe that when He [God] said this He was not
> expressing a sentiment but stating a fact—just as one is stating a

fact when one says that a lock and its key are one mechanism, or that a violin and a bow are one musical instrument. The inventor of the human machine was telling us that its two halves, the male and the female, were made to be combined together in pairs, not simply on the sexual level, but totally combined.[10]

But unity doesn't come naturally. We nod in agreement when the pastor says the words "and the two shall become one flesh," but many people waltz down the aisle, walk out the door, and try to decide "which one." Many snuff out the candles representing their separate lives and light the unity candle, and then begin the process of snuffing out each other. But God makes it clear that marriage is the melding of two hearts into one, two lives into one.

The landmark of prayer for your marriage is your husband's ring finger. Not everyone wears a wedding ring, but surveys show that 85 percent of married men and 91.7 percent of married women do.[11] The wedding ring holds great symbolism, and I, for one, am glad my husband keeps his securely in place.

The circle of the ring has no beginning and no end and represents never-ending love. It is a symbol of the couple's promise to be faithful to one another "until death do us part." The wedding ring is traditionally worn on the fourth finger of the left hand. This tradition began with the Romans who believed that a vein ran directly from this finger right to the heart.[12]

We're going to approach this landmark of prayer a little differently than the others. Since marriage involves both of you, you'll be praying for your husband's role in marriage and yours as well. A few verses are specifically selected for your husband, but most of them will apply to both you and your man.

As you pray for your husband's ring finger, you'll be praying for your marriage to be a God-honoring union of man and wife as two become one.

His Side: *His Relationships*

I've often thought I could be a stellar Christian if I just didn't have to deal with people! Sometimes they just make life so difficult. But God created people to live in relationship, to live in community. Iron sharpening iron. Heart loving heart. Hand helping hand.

When Jesus walked the earth in human flesh, He did so in the context of relationships. He could have accomplished God's redemptive plan all by Himself. He did not need one other human soul to carry out the miracles, messages, and ministry of those thirty-three and a half years. And yet He chose to live in relationship with others—people who often made His life on earth more difficult. He lived in a family who often did not understand Him (Mark 3:20–21, 31–34), in a community that often did not accept Him (Mark 6:1–6), and with a bunch of men who often did not believe Him (Matthew 16:21–23).

Jesus ministered to the multitudes, but He also had a close relationship with seventy-two followers, a closer relationship with a group of twelve, and a heart-to-heart connection with three: Peter, James, and John. Even then, it was His heavenly Father with whom Jesus communed on the most intimate level in moment-by-moment abiding.

God never intended for man to walk this earth in isolation. Only a few moments after man's grand debut on the sixth day of creation, God said, "It is not good for the man to be alone" (Genesis 2:18). And in creating the fabulous Eve, He placed Adam right smack-dab in the middle of community.

Father, mother, sisters, brothers, aunts, uncles, sons, daughters, friends, bosses, employees, coworkers, neighbors, and the list goes on. Your man is surrounded by relationships that can affect him for good or for bad.

Have you ever been around someone for an extended period of time and the next thing you know you sound like them, talk like them, act like them? When I go back to my hometown for a visit, I come back with a heavier southern twang (yes, that is possible). When I spend time with my friend Gwen, I come home talking a little more "hip" than before. When I go to Canada, I come home ending every sentence with "eh?" We are sponges, soaking up the personas of those with whom we walk side by side. The people with whom your husband spends his time affect his attitudes, character, behavior, speech, and outlook on life. Relationships are the change agents God uses to sand away the rough edges of our personalities and shore up the weak places of the soul.

As you pray for your husband's side, you'll be praying for his relationships, friendships, and partnerships—the people who influence his actions, his attitudes, his character, and his future.

His Sexuality: *His Need for Physical Intimacy*

It seems all too often that we hear of yet another godly man caught in the trap of sexual sin. I don't know about you, but I grow weary hearing stories of men drawn away and enticed into extramarital affairs, pornography, and carnal immorality.

Satan has done a masterful job of taking something God created for good and perverting it in ways never intended. Bible teacher Beth Moore wrote:

> Satan's attacks on sexuality have become so outright and blatant that we're becoming frighteningly desensitized and are unknowingly readjusting the plumb line to a state of relativity. In other words, instead of measuring our lives against the goal of Christlikeness, we are beginning to subconsciously measure our lives against the world's depravity.... Satan is increasing the dosage of sexually immoral provocation with such consistency that we don't realize how much poison we're swallowing.[13]

First of all, let me say that sex was God's idea. He went through a lot of trouble to create all the intricacies that make sex enjoyable and fulfilling for both a man and a woman. However, when that union is not under the protective canopy of marriage between one man and one woman, perversion and shame taint the intended beauty. Sex outside of a monogamous, heterosexual union between husband and wife becomes a soul-rotting, guilt-ridden sin that eats away at the heart like nothing else ever could.

Satan has access to our husbands like never before. In times past, a man had to publicly walk into a store and make a purchase in order to look at pornography. Now all he has to do is sit in the quiet of his own white-picket-fence home, click a few buttons on his computer, and a landfill of images magically appear. Satan entices men to take a quick peek, then traps them in secret shame as they fall captive to a miserable life of deception and addiction.

The Enemy has launched an all-out war against God's precious gift of sexual intimacy. We need to fight for our husbands on our knees. But first, we need to consider the other side of the coin.

This is one area of our husbands' lives where our choices wield great influence. Before I wrote the book *Becoming the Woman of His Dreams,* I interviewed and surveyed hundreds of men from all walks of life to discover seven qualities a man longs for in a wife. I'm sure it won't surprise you that sexual fulfillment and respect were at the top of the list.

Women and men approach sex from different perspectives. You already knew that, right? For a woman, sexual desire is stirred by a man's display of affection, attention, and adoration. For a man, affection, attention, and adoration are stirred by sex with his wife. A woman wants to feel cherished by her man. A man wants to feel desired by his woman.

Sexual fulfillment is a physical *and* emotional need for a man. Emotional? Yes, emotional. He won't describe it that way. He may not even understand the correlation. But when a husband's sex life is good, it gives him the confidence to excel in other areas of his life. Sexual fulfillment unlocks a man's emotions, and you, dear wife, hold the key.

If you pray for your husband from head to toe but neglect to fulfill his sexual needs, you are undermining the very protection and success you're praying for. It reminds me of what James described: "If a brother or sister is without clothing and in need of daily food, and one of you says to them, 'Go in peace, be warmed and be filled,' and yet you do not give them what is necessary for their body, what use is that?" (James 2:15–16, NASB). This is one area where our prayers must join with an active commitment to "give them what is necessary for their body."

For most wives, it's not that they don't care about the sexual aspect of marriage. It's that the cares of life tend to push physical intimacy down the priority list. Let's face it: being a woman is hard work! So many other demands scream for our attention. We have children to raise, a house to clean, groceries to stock, meals to cook, a job to perform, and the list goes on. But, sister, I encourage you to keep your man at the top of the list, right under your relationship with God. Don't relegate him to the sidelines until the children are older and think he is going to stand by patiently waiting for you to notice him.

Why make sex a priority in your marriage? Paul says that sexual intimacy "unites" the two participants. The Greek word for "unite" is *kollao,* meaning "to glue together, to make cohere."[14] Sex is not just the glue of marriage. It is the superglue.

But your husband longs for more than the physical act. He wants to be wanted—by you. What he doesn't want is halfhearted accommodation. If you engage in sex because you see it as your wifely duty, then he'll know it. He would rather reroof a house in 101-degree heat than "make love" to a wife who is responding out of duty. He might feel a physical release when the song is sung, but he will not feel fulfilled or satisfied in his heart.

If you are not meeting your husband's sexual needs, then everything you say to him is perceived through a lens of rejection. You may think the sexual part of your marriage will improve once the other areas of his life are in order, but I can assure you, he thinks the opposite. To him, the other areas of your marriage will improve when your sex life is in order.

You may be tempted to pray your husband would think less about sex, but you won't find support for that in the Scriptures. God hard-wired a man's brain to care deeply about this aspect of his life. I'm not sure what God was thinking when He created man and woman so differently in this area, but it sure does make the adventure of marriage interesting.

As you pray for your husband's sexuality, you'll be praying for him to have strength to resist temptation, find fulfillment in the marriage bed, and experience continued or renewed passion in your lovemaking that will leave him feeling like the king of the hill. And while you're praying, join God in His work by meeting your man's sexual needs with renewed enthusiasm, joy, and delight.

His Legs: *His Stand on the Truth*

When I was in grade school, I learned that Pluto was the ninth planet in our solar system. In 2006 scientists said, "Oops, it's not really a planet after all." It was downgraded to "dwarf planet" status and bumped off the list of nine planets that revolve around our sun. I envisioned thousands of schoolchildren plucking the brownish-orange orb from their science project displays. Just another truth that wasn't true after all.

In our modern culture ideas and ideals that were supposedly true yesterday are declared false today. What's right today may be wrong tomorrow, and what's illegal today may be legal tomorrow. Modern man echoes Pilate's words to Jesus, "What is truth?" (John 18:38).

We live in a world where relativism is embraced, a culture that says all points of view are equally valid and all truth is relative to the individual. People say things like, "That may be true for you, but that doesn't mean it is true for me." Of course that is ridiculous. If a truth can change depending on perspective, place, or time, then it is not true at all. This mind-set mirrors that of the Israelites during the time of the Judges: "Everyone did what was right in his own eyes" (Judges 17:6; 21:25, NASB).

But as God has shown us time and time again, truth is an exclusive reality, not an elusive myth. There is a truth that transcends culture and individual inclinations. And that truth is Jesus Christ.

Jesus said, "I am the way and the truth and the life" (John 14:6). "The Word [Jesus] became flesh and made his dwelling among us. We have seen his glory, the glory of the one and only Son, who came from the Father, full of grace and truth" (John 1:14, NIV 2011). Jesus repeatedly started His teachings with the words "I tell you the truth" or "truly I say to you" (John 5:19, 24–25; 6:26, 32, 53). He is the Truth and the Source of truth.

So what does all this have to do with praying for the landmark of your husband's legs? Everything. Your man needs to *stand* on the Truth. Everything else is shifting sand. If he does not stand on the Truth, the world becomes a confusing place where the undertow of uncertainty will pull him out to sea with a riptide of questions and the shifting tides of change. As God told the Israelites, "If you do not stand firm in your faith, you will not stand at all" (Isaiah 7:9).

And that is a message for all of us. If we do not *stand* on the Truth, then we will not *stand* at all. We will be tossed back and forth like a spineless rag doll by a childlike world that pitches a fit to get its own way.

As you pray for your husband's legs, you'll be praying he will stand firm in his faith in a wishy-washy world. You'll be praying he will stand on the unchanging, infallible truth of God.

His Knees: *His Relationship with God*

For twenty-eight years Barbara prayed that her husband, Tim, would come to know Jesus as Savior and Lord. "That's just not for me," he'd say when she invited him to church with her. "You go on ahead."

Barbara continued praying.

One Easter, Tim surprised his wife by agreeing to attend church. "I'm only going to do this once," he said. "I've got this suit on, and I'm going with you because it's Easter. But this is a one-time deal. Don't ask me to go again."

She didn't need to ask again. During the service, God moved Tim's heart in such a powerful way that he was down the aisle and at the altar before the pastor finished the invitation. Now this country carpenter has dedicated his life to building houses for a nonprofit and telling others about Jesus, who plucked him from the flames of hell and set his feet on the path to eternal life. The man loves Jesus.

And his wife still prays, confident that God hears.

Knees. That is the landmark that brings you to praying for your husband's relationship with God. Bending his knees in humility breaks the chains of pride and sets him truly free to experience the abundant life on earth and eternal life in heaven that Jesus came to give.

James reminds us: "Humble yourselves in the sight of the Lord, and He will lift you up" (James 4:10, NKJV). The Amplified Bible puts it this way: "Humble yourselves [feeling very insignificant] in the presence of the Lord, and He will exalt you [He will lift you up and make your lives significant]."

The opposite of humility is pride. Webster's defines *pride* as "excessive self-esteem." It is a type of self-worship that takes full credit for one's accomplishments, resources, and successes. Pride was what caused Satan to fall from heaven (Ezekiel 28), Saul to lose his reign over Israel (1 Samuel 13), and King Uzziah to be cursed with leprosy (2 Chronicles 26:16–22). Pride makes a man refuse to bend the knee in submission to God, stunts his spiritual growth, and stymies his passion for Christ.

As you pray for your husband's knees, you'll be praying for him to humbly kneel in submission to God, in worship of God, and in communion with God. You'll also be praying against pride that prevents him from doing so.

His Feet: *His Walk*

Rachel and I sat on weatherworn steps leading down to a pristine beach. We had a front-row seat as the morning sun stretched its arms over the horizon. She was hurting. I was attempting to love her back to health.

Salty air. Salty ocean. Salt-of-the-earth friend. It is hard to beat that combination when you're soul sick.

Rachel's life had taken some unexpected turns. Let me rephrase that. It wasn't that her life "had taken" some unexpected turns, as if she had nothing to do with it. She had strayed from God's path, and *she* had taken some unexpected turns. She had given in to sexual temptation and, as a result, had lost her marriage, the trust of her children, and many of her friends. She had lost her true self.

As we sat on the bottom step with our toes buried in the cool sand, we stared out at the glassy ocean and pristine beach. It was as if Jesus had spoken, "Peace, be still," and the wind and waves obeyed. The sand, airbrushed smooth by the night breeze, had not yet been disturbed by vacationers' feet, kids' buckets, and sunbathers' chairs.

Rachel spotted a set of tire tracks running close to the water's edge. Four shallow ruts. Parallel indentations. Ruts that never deviated in distance one from the other, as far as the eye could see. If one swerved, they all swerved in union.

"I wish life were like that," she whispered.

"Like what?" I asked.

"Like those tire tracks," she replied. "Us and God. Me and God. Always moving in tandem. Side by side. Hooked together. Moving in the same direction. Connected. Easy. Perfectly aligned."

We sat in silence, staring at the tracks, both knowing the reason her tracks had deviated from God's. She had detached herself from the Master chassis and made tracks of her own. She had willingly let go of God's hand and walked away.

The Christian life is often referred to as our spiritual walk. "Walk by faith, not by sight," Paul encouraged the Corinthian church (2 Corinthians 5:7, NASB). The New International Version translates this same verse, "We live by faith, not by sight."

Paul wrote to the Galatians, "I say then: Walk in the Spirit, and you shall not fulfill the lust of the flesh.... If we live in the Spirit, let us also walk in the Spirit" (Galatians 5:16, 25, NKJV). Again, the New International Version translates these same words: "So I say, live by the Spirit, and you will not gratify the desires of the sinful nature.... Since we live by the Spirit, let us keep in step with the Spirit." I love the idea of *keeping in step* with the Holy Spirit. What a wonderful way to live: walking in step and keeping time with the Holy Spirit's pace.

Your husband faces decisions throughout his day that determine whether he will walk in tandem with Jesus or in sync with the world. Steps become a lifestyle; a lifestyle becomes a legacy.

So as you come to this final landmark of prayer—your husband's feet—you'll be praying for where his feet take him on the journey of life, what paths he chooses along the way, and how he keeps in step with God.

Now that we've covered the landmarks of prayer, let's begin the exciting adventure of praying for your husband from head to toe. "When a believing person prays, great things happen" (James 5:16, NCV). I am so excited just thinking about the great things that are going to happen with your marriage and in your man.

Part 2

Thirty Days of Praying
Scripture over
Your Husband from
Head to Toe

Day One

His Mind

> Do not let this Book of the Law depart from your mouth; meditate on it day and night, so that you may be careful to do everything written in it. Then you will be prosperous and successful. *Joshua 1:8*

Heavenly Father, I pray my husband will meditate on Your Word day and night so that he may be careful to do everything written in it. I ask that the Holy Spirit bring certain verses or passages to his mind throughout the day. Stir him to ponder the words and consider what You are saying to him. Make Your Truth the plumb line to show him any thoughts that are crooked or out of alignment with Your Word. I pray You will make him prosperous and successful as he applies the principles of Scripture to his life.

His Eyes

> When the woman saw that the fruit of the tree was good for food and pleasing to the eye, and also desirable for gaining wisdom, she took some and ate it. She also gave some to her husband, who was with her, and he ate it. *Genesis 3:6*

Keep my husband from looking at anything or anyone that would tempt him to sin. Give him the desire and the willpower to turn away and resist the lure of temporary pleasures that have lasting effects on his earthly life.

His Ears

> You have declared this day that the LORD is your God and that you will walk in obedience to him, that you will keep his decrees, commands and laws—that you will listen to him. *Deuteronomy 26:17,* NIV 2011

Dear God, help my husband keep Your decrees, obey Your commands, and listen to Your voice speaking to his heart. Shut his ears to the voices of the world, the flesh, the devil, and anything that would lead him astray. Attune his ears to voices that are consistent with Your teaching and Your Word.

His Mouth

> May the words of my mouth...be *pleasing* in your sight, O LORD, my Rock and my Redeemer. *Psalm 19:14*

I pray the words of my husband's mouth will be pleasing in Your sight, O Lord, his Rock and his Redeemer. May his conversation be fitting for a child of God and representative of Christ in the world.

His Neck

> So give your servant a discerning heart to govern your people and to distinguish between right and wrong. *1 Kings 3:9*

Lord, just as King Solomon prayed for discernment, I ask that You help my husband distinguish between right and wrong. Help him choose Your best in every situation.

His Shoulders

> Is anything too hard for the LORD? *Genesis 18:14*

No matter what my husband has to go through today, assure him that nothing is too hard for You. Empower him to cut the cords of worry with the saber of praise and to place his burdens on Your able shoulders.

His Heart

> May...the meditation of my heart be pleasing in your sight, O LORD, my Rock and my Redeemer. *Psalm 19:14*

I pray that the meditations of my husband's heart will be pleasing in Your sight. Make the wellspring of his heart pure so that what flows from it will be honorable, reputable, and upright.

His Back

For the LORD your God moves around in your camp to protect you and to defeat your enemies. *Deuteronomy 23:14,* NLT

Almighty God, I ask that You move about in my husband's camp—his home, his workplace, and everywhere in between. Protect him and deliver him from any who would seek to do him harm.

His Arms

The LORD is my strength and my song; he has become my salvation. *Exodus 15:2*

O Lord, be my husband's strength, song, and sure defense. Empower him to do all You have called him to do today. Be his strength for every struggle and his victory song for every battle.

His Hands

When his master saw that the LORD was with him and that the LORD gave him success in everything he did, Joseph found favor in his eyes and became his attendant.
Genesis 39:3–4

Lord, just as Joseph's master saw that You were with him and that You gave him success in everything he did, I pray my husband's coworkers will see that You are with him and that You give him success. May he find favor in his field of employment and recognize that favor as Your blessing on his life and in his work.

His Ring Finger

> The LORD God said, "It is not good for the man to be alone.
> I will make a helper suitable for him." *Genesis 2:18*

Lord, make me a helper to my husband and not a hindrance, a completer and not a competer, a chief cheerleader and not a chief critic. I pray my husband will see me as his God-ordained partner. I commit to be the type of helper You have fashioned me to be: a woman who seeks to love, honor, and respect her husband for the rest of our lives.

His Side

> Honor your father and your mother, as the LORD your God
> has commanded you, so that you may live long and that it
> may go well with you in the land the LORD your God is giving
> you. *Deuteronomy 5:16*

I lift up my husband's relationship with his parents. Help him to honor and respect his father and mother, so that he will have a long, full life. Give him grace to forgive them for the times they have let him down and a grateful heart to appreciate them for the times they have encouraged him on. May he respect them and value their investment in his life.

His Sexuality

> [Then] the LORD God formed the man from the dust of the ground
> and breathed into his nostrils the breath of life, and the man
> became a living being. *Genesis 2:7*

Heavenly Father, thank You for the meticulous way You created and fashioned my husband's body for physical intimacy. Bless our sex life so that he will be fulfilled, content, and self-assured. Help me to be the wife he needs to satisfy his sexual longings.

His Legs

> Moses answered the people, "Do not be afraid. Stand firm and
> you will see the deliverance the LORD will bring you today....
> The LORD will fight for you; you need only to be still."
> *Exodus 14:13–14*

Strengthen my husband's courage and confidence in You so that he will not be afraid when trials and difficulties shake his world. Just as the Israelites stood firm to witness Your deliverance and rescue, empower him to stand firm in his faith to witness You working in his life. Help him not to worry and fret but to rest secure in the knowledge of Your protection and provision.

His Knees

> Come, let us bow down in worship, let us kneel before the LORD
> our Maker; for he is our God and we are the people of his pasture,
> the flock under his care. *Psalm 95:6–7*

Lord God, give my husband a humble spirit that willingly bows down in worship of You and kneels in adoration before You. Help him to remember that You are his Maker and he is a sheep in Your pasture, a lamb under Your tender care.

His Feet

> Enoch walked with God.... Noah...walked with God. *Genesis 5:24; 6:9*

Heavenly Father, keep my husband on the right path today. May he be known as a man who walks with You. Lead him. Guide him. Show him Your way. Father, don't let him run ahead of You or lag behind You; instead, encourage and enable him to walk steadily in tandem with You. In Jesus' name, amen.

Day Two

His Mind

Test me, O LORD, and try me, examine my heart and my mind; for your love is ever before me, and I walk continually in your truth. *Psalm 26:2–3*

All-wise God, examine my husband's mind to reveal any thoughts that are contrary to Your truth. Please root out any thoughts that are counter-productive to godly living. Give him an awareness of Your unfailing love for him. Help him recognize any lies of the Enemy that would cause him to doubt Your love and replace those lies with the truth.

His Eyes

And don't let us yield to temptation. *Luke 11:4,* NLT

Strengthen my husband's resolve to resist the temptation to look at any person or image of a person that would cause him to sin in his heart. Give him the determination to divert his eyes quickly and the willpower to look the other way.

His Ears

Speak, for your servant is listening. *1 Samuel 3:10*

Lord, increase my husband's sensitivity to Your still small voice speaking to his inner man. May he listen intently, carefully, and attentively to all You have to say.

His Mouth

Then they despised the pleasant land; they did not believe his promise. They grumbled in their tents and did not obey the LORD. *Psalm 106:24–25*

No matter what this day brings, keep my husband from grumbling or complaining. Help him to see the many ways You have blessed him, and prompt him to give thanks in all things. I pray his words will not block Your promises from being manifested in his life but instead open the floodgates of heaven with blessings outpoured.

His Neck

Do not be stiff-necked, as your fathers were; submit to the LORD.

2 Chronicles 30:8

Lord, deliver my husband from any tendencies to be stiff-necked, stubborn, or determined to do things his own way. Stir up in him a desire to base his choices on Your will, Your direction, and Your Word.

His Shoulders

The LORD himself goes before you and will be with you; he will never leave you nor forsake you. Do not be afraid; do not be discouraged.

Deuteronomy 31:8

Lord, please remind my husband that You go before him and are always with him; that You will never leave him or forsake him. Strengthen his faith so that he will not be afraid of what the future holds or discouraged when circumstances do not turn out the way he had hoped. Help him trust in Your sovereign plan.

His Heart

Delight yourself in the LORD and he will give you the desires of your heart. *Psalm 37:4*

Lord, fill my husband with heavenly joy, and move him to delight in Your presence. Infuse his heart with Your desires so that they will become his desires.

His Back

[David said,] "The LORD who delivered me from the paw of the lion and the paw of the bear will deliver me from the hand of this Philistine."

1 Samuel 17:37

Almighty Lord, just as You protected David from the paw of the lion, the paw of the bear, and the threats of Goliath, I pray You will protect my husband from those who would rise up to do him harm. Make him a man of courage who knows You will protect him in any battle You have called him to face. Help him not be afraid of those who appear to be bigger, stronger, or more powerful than him, but to be confident in Your all-encompassing protection and all-sufficient power to save.

His Arms

The LORD gave this command to Joshua son of Nun: "Be strong and courageous, for you will bring the Israelites into the land I promised them on oath, and I myself will be with you." *Deuteronomy 31:23*

Empower my husband to be strong and courageous as he does the work You have called him to do. Prompt him to take hold of the mighty promises in Your Word.

His Hands

Then Moses said to the Israelites, "See, the LORD has chosen Bezalel son of Uri, the son of Hur, of the tribe of Judah, and he has filled him with the Spirit of God, with skill, ability and knowledge in all kinds of crafts—to make artistic designs for work in gold, silver and bronze, to cut and set stones, to work in wood and to engage in all kinds of artistic craftsmanship." *Exodus 35:30–33*

Just as You empowered and equipped Bezalel to do work that was beyond his training and experience, I ask that You will fill my husband with Your

Spirit and give him skills and abilities to perform his tasks in the workplace. Bless him with ingenuity and expertise that are beyond his training, experience, and education so that he will bring glory to Your name.

His Ring Finger

The man said, "This is now bone of my bones and flesh of my flesh; she shall be called 'woman,' for she was taken out of man." For this reason a man will leave his father and mother and be united to his wife, and they will become one flesh. *Genesis 2:23–24*

Help my husband and me to put our marriage above all other earthly relationships. Give us the courage and commitment to leave and cleave by keeping our family unit a priority over extended family relationships, even if it upsets others. While we seek to honor our mother and father on both sides of the family, show us how to protect our marriage from any influences of extended family members that would threaten our unity. Help us draw clear boundaries that protect, nurture, and strengthen our marriage.

His Side

How good and pleasant it is when brothers live together in unity! It is like precious oil poured on the head, running down on the beard, running down on Aaron's beard, down upon the collar of his robes. *Psalm 133:1–2*

I pray my husband will enjoy living in unity with his friends, family, and coworkers. Protect him from wrong relationships or difficult situations that would block Your blessings from flowing like oil from the top of his head to the tips of his toes.

His Sexuality

Now Joseph was well-built and handsome, and after a while his master's wife took notice of Joseph and said, "Come to bed with me!"

> But he refused.... "How then could I do such a wicked thing and sin
> against God?" *Genesis 39:6–9*

Fill my husband with the courage and conviction to be like young Joseph, who resisted sexual temptation and ran in the opposite direction. Remind him that such an offense is not just a sin against me but more important, against You. Protect him from seduction of every kind, and deliver him from the evil enticements of this world.

His Legs

> The priests who carried the ark of the covenant of the LORD stood firm
> on dry ground in the middle of the Jordan, while all Israel passed by until
> the whole nation had completed the crossing on dry ground. *Joshua 3:17*

Give my husband the faith to stand firm in the center of Your will, fully expecting You to perform miracles, wonders, and mighty acts on his behalf.

His Knees

> If you are pleased with me, teach me your ways so I may know you and
> continue to find favor with you. *Exodus 33:13*

Blessed Father, make my husband a man who humbles himself before You, learns from You, and finds favor with You. Stir up a desire in his heart to know You, Lord, not just intellectually but relationally. May he be a devoted disciple and a faithful follower, bending his knee in humble adoration and submission to You.

His Feet

> Walk in all the way that the LORD your God has commanded you, so
> that you may live and prosper and prolong your days in the land that
> you will possess. *Deuteronomy 5:33*

Father, may Your Spirit guide my husband to walk in the way You have commanded him so that he may live and prosper and prolong his days. Hem him in so that he will not veer to the right or the left but will keep his feet on the path You have marked out for him. In Jesus' name, amen.

Day Three

His Mind

On my bed I remember you; I think of you through the watches of the night. *Psalm 63:6*

Almighty God, I pray my husband will think of You throughout the day and into the night. Make his last thoughts before falling asleep be of You, and may thoughts of You permeate even his dreams.

His Eyes

When the LORD saw that he had gone over to look, God called to him from within the bush, "Moses! Moses!" And Moses said, "Here I am." *Exodus 3:4*

Help my husband see You today. Prompt him to turn aside from what he is doing and recognize Your presence in his life. Open his eyes to see You in extraordinary and ordinary moments of sudden glory when You make Yourself known to him in personal ways.

His Ears

The LORD warned Israel and Judah through all his prophets and seers: "Turn from your evil ways. Observe my commands and decrees, in accordance with the entire Law that I commanded your fathers to obey and that I delivered to you through my servants the prophets." But they would not listen and were as stiff-necked as their fathers, who did not trust in the LORD their God. *2 Kings 17:13–14*

Lord, keep my husband from being like the stiff-necked, rebellious Isra-elites who did not trust You or listen to You. Teach him instead to be quick to listen and to obey Your commands. Prompt him to turn his ear away from any evil influences and toward all godly influences. Help him to not listen to any music, media, or man that would undermine his trust in You.

His Mouth

Our mouths were filled with laughter, our tongues with songs of joy. Then it was said among the nations, "The LORD has done great things for them." *Psalm 126:2*

Loving Father, fill my husband's mouth with laughter and his tongue with songs of joy. Let the words of his mouth cause others to say, "The Lord has done great things for him." I pray his speech will bubble over with gratitude so that others will want to know the Source of his deep-seated joy.

His Neck

You warned them to return to your law, but they became arrogant and disobeyed your commands. They sinned against your ordinances, by which a man will live if he obeys them. Stubbornly they turned their backs on you, became stiff-necked and refused to listen. *Nehemiah 9:29*

Lord, remove any arrogance, stubbornness, or pride from my husband's heart that would cause him to make decisions based on selfish desires rather than Your desires. Make him humble, submissive, and eager to do Your will and follow Your ways. Let Scripture be the plumb line against which he measures every decision and the scales on which he weighs every choice.

His Shoulders

Those who know your name will trust in you, for you, LORD, have never forsaken those who seek you. *Psalm 9:10*

Thank You, Lord, that You never forsake those who seek You. Lift any burdens of worry or anxiety from my husband's shoulders. Teach him to rest in, lean on, and confidently put his trust in You.

His Heart

Create in me a pure heart, O God, and renew a steadfast spirit within me. *Psalm 51:10*

Loving Lord, make my husband's heart pure. Clean it up and clean it out by the power of Your Holy Spirit. Renew a steadfast and secure spirit within him. Breathe a fresh anointing of Your Holy Spirit into his life today.

His Back

"Don't be afraid," the prophet answered. "Those who are with us are more than those who are with them." *2 Kings 6:16*

Lord, just as the prophet Elisha was confident that the warring angels surrounding him were greater than the enemy who sought to do him harm, I pray my husband will be confident that Your power surrounding him is greater than anyone or anything that might seek to do him harm. Even though he may not see Your mighty host, reassure him that he is under Your protective care.

His Arms

Be strong and courageous. Do not be afraid or terrified because of them, for the LORD your God goes with you; he will never leave you nor forsake you. *Deuteronomy 31:6*

Thank You for the promise that You will never leave nor forsake my husband. Strengthen him when he is weak, bolster his courage when he is afraid, and reassure him when he doubts. Remind him that You, Lord God, go with him to protect and deliver him from trouble.

His Hands

> Do not use dishonest standards when measuring length, weight or quantity. Use honest scales and honest weights, an honest ephah and an honest hin. *Leviticus 19:35–36*

Guide my husband to be completely honest and hold to high standards in his work today. May he resist any temptation to overcharge or underdeliver but instead treat every individual with absolute integrity.

His Ring Finger

> Search me, O God, and know my heart; test me and know my anxious thoughts. See if there is any offensive way in me, and lead me in the way everlasting. *Psalm 139:23–24*

Heavenly Father, it is so easy to allow bitterness, resentment, and anger to creep into marriage. Please search my heart and my husband's heart. Show us anything in our lives that is potentially destructive or detrimental to our marriage. Help us root out any harmful patterns and behaviors we've developed over time, and lead us in the way of a God-honoring and God-centered marriage.

His Side

> The righteous should choose his friends carefully, for the way of the wicked leads them astray. *Proverbs 12:26,* NKJV

Heavenly Father, give my husband a discerning spirit and intuitive heart so that he will choose his friends carefully. Help him build relationships that will foster godly character and avoid those that would lead him astray.

His Sexuality

> The man and his wife were both naked, and they felt no shame.
> *Genesis 2:25*

I pray my husband will feel no shame in his sexual desires but see them as a gift from You to be enjoyed between husband and wife. Remove any feelings of shame from past sexual sin and renew a healthy perspective of Your precious plan for marriage. May he view his sexuality as yet another reason to praise You for Your creative genius and divine care.

His Legs

> Choose for yourselves this day whom you will serve.... But as for me
> and my household, we will serve the LORD. *Joshua 24:15*

No matter what anyone else around him is doing or saying, give my husband a righteous determination to take a firm stand of faith. May he rise up and say, through his actions as well as his words, "As for me and my household, we will serve the Lord."

His Knees

> When pride comes, then comes disgrace, but with humility comes
> wisdom. *Proverbs 11:2*

Remove any pride from my husband that would make him falsely think that he could make life work on his own. Help him to bend his knee in humility so that You can place a crown of wisdom on his head. Bless his contrite spirit with godly wisdom, virtuous character, and great success.

His Feet

> Observe the commands of the LORD your God, walking in his ways
> and revering him. *Deuteronomy 8:6*

O Lord Most High, stir up a desire in my husband to observe Your commands, walk in Your ways, and revere Your holiness. Keep him from veering off Your path. Place a hedge of protection on his left and right so that he will stay on the road You have marked out for him. In Jesus' name, amen.

Day Four

His Mind

> You will keep in perfect peace him whose mind is steadfast, because
> he trusts in you. *Isaiah 26:3*

Dear Lord, keep my husband's mind steadfast, focused, and settled on You so that he can experience perfect peace. Deliver him from any thoughts that keep him tangled up in anxious fretting or tied up with weighty concerns. As he places his trust in You, loosen the knots of worry and unbind the burdens of care.

His Eyes

> I will set before my eyes no vile thing. *Psalm 101:3*

Turn my husband's eyes away from anything vile or vulgar. Don't let his eyes be captured by curiosity, but give him the conviction and resolve to quickly look away from anything that would cause him to sin in his heart. Help him resist the impulse to look at pornography or any image that would stir up lustful thoughts. Strengthen his determination to click the Delete key, change the television channel, and walk away from visually tempting images or people.

His Ears

> For God does speak—now one way, now another—though
> man may not perceive it. In a dream, in a vision of the night,
> when deep sleep falls on men as they slumber in their beds,
> he may speak in their ears and terrify them with warnings,
> to turn man from wrongdoing and keep him from pride.
> *Job 33:14–17*

Gracious God, tune my husband's spiritual ears to the frequency of Your voice. I pray he will not put You in a box but be open to the various ways You can and do speak to him. Whether dreaming at night, driving in his car, riding on the bus, waiting for a client, making a delivery, hammering a nail, sitting at his desk, or standing in a checkout line, I pray he will be spiritually sensitive to Your still small voice speaking to his inner man.

His Mouth

> Set a guard over my mouth, O LORD; keep watch over the door of my lips. *Psalm 141:3*

Set a guard over my husband's mouth, O Lord, and keep watch over the door of his lips. Don't let any unwise or ungodly word slip into his conversation.

His Neck

> Who, then, is the man that fears the LORD? He will instruct him in the way chosen for him. *Psalm 25:12*

Lord Most High, make my husband a man who honors, respects, and reveres You at all times. Let him fear You alone and seek to please You above all else. I pray You will guide him in all his decisions and that he will follow Your instructions to a T.

His Shoulders

> But I trust in your unfailing love; my heart rejoices in your salvation. I will sing to the LORD, for he has been good to me. *Psalm 13:5–6*

Remind my husband of Your unfailing love for him and Your incredible gift of salvation given to him. May he rejoice as he recalls the many blessings You have showered on his life. Free him from the shackles of worry with the key of gratitude. Strengthen his faith as he remembers all the ways You have been good to him.

His Heart

> My heart is steadfast, O God, my heart is steadfast; I will sing and make music. *Psalm 57:7*

I pray my husband's heart will be confident and secure in who he is in Christ, what he has in Christ, and where he is in Christ. Remove any feelings of inferiority, insecurity, or inadequacy that would threaten to hold him back and replace them with a God-confidence that will propel him to move ahead. Put a song of praise and victory in his heart today.

His Back

> He [Nebuchadnezzar] said, "Look! I see four men walking around in the fire, unbound and unharmed, and the fourth looks like a son of the gods." *Daniel 3:25*

Gracious God, just as you protected Shadrach, Meshach, and Abednego in Nebuchadnezzar's fiery furnace, protect my husband from harm. No matter how hot the circumstances he has to walk through today, deliver him unscathed and unscarred, without even a hint of smoke. May Jesus' protecting presence be evident to him and to those watching his life.

His Arms

> Have I not commanded you? Be strong and courageous. Do not be terrified; do not be discouraged, for the LORD your God will be with you wherever you go. *Joshua 1:9*

Empower my husband with Your Spirit so he will be strong and courageous as he goes through his day. Protect him from discouragement and fear by reminding him You are with him wherever he goes. Show him Your power as You fight for him, defend him, and deliver him from harm.

His Hands

Bless all his skills, O LORD, and be pleased with the work of his hands.

Deuteronomy 33:11

Dear Lord, bless my husband's skills and be pleased with the work of his hands. Reward his efforts and bring him success. Thank You for giving him gifts and talents. May he use those abilities to glorify You.

His Ring Finger

Two are better than one, because they have a good return for their work: If one falls down, his friend can help him up. But pity the man who falls and has no one to help him up!

Ecclesiastes 4:9–10

Lord, thank You that my husband and I have each other. Bind our hearts together so that we can help each other up when we fall and celebrate with each other when we succeed. Remove any sense of competition, contention, or one-upmanship, and show us how to live in unity as man and wife as You intended. Help us to be a tightly braided cord of three strands intertwined with You.

His Side

A generous man will prosper; he who refreshes others will himself be refreshed. *Proverbs 11:25*

Gracious God, prompt my husband to be a generous man. Move him to use his resources, time, words, and actions to refresh friends, family, and coworkers. As he pours himself into the lives of others, renew him with the living water of Jesus Christ.

His Sexuality

Sin is crouching at the door, eager to control you. But you must subdue it and be its master. *Genesis 4:7*, NLT

If my husband hears the knock of temptation on the door of his heart, give him the wisdom, willpower, and unyielding determination not to open the door or even look through the peephole. Deliver him from temptation, and give him the power to subdue it and master it.

His Legs

It is God who arms me with strength and makes my way perfect. He makes my feet like the feet of a deer; he enables me to stand on the heights. *2 Samuel 22:33–34*

Almighty God, strengthen my husband's stand for truth, and keep his way secure. Help him stand firm in his faith, even when others around him teeter on the cliff of uncertainty. Support him so he can remain upright on the heights of moral character as he navigates the rocky terrain of this wavering world.

His Knees

He mocks proud mockers but gives grace to the humble. *Proverbs 3:34*

I pray my husband will humbly submit his entire life to Your sovereign rule and righteous reign. Remove any sense of pride that would keep him from bending his knee in humility, and remind him of the many ways You have heaped grace upon his life.

His Feet

And now, O Israel, what does the LORD your God ask of you but to fear the LORD your God, to walk in all his ways, to love him, to serve the LORD your God with all your heart and with all your soul, and to

observe the LORD's commands and decrees that I am giving you today
for your own good? *Deuteronomy 10:12–13*

Holy Lord, may my husband fear You with a holy reverence and walk in Your righteous ways. May he love You, serve You, and observe Your commands with all his heart and with all his soul. Help him to see obedience not as something he has to do, but as something he gets to do, knowing that Your commands are for his own good. In Jesus' name, amen.

Day Five

His Mind

Yet this I call to mind and therefore I have hope: Because of the LORD's great love we are not consumed, for his compassions never fail. They are new every morning; great is your faithfulness.

Lamentations 3:21–23

Dear Lord, remind my husband of Your great love for him today. Help him remember that Your compassions never fail and that Your mercies are new every morning. Awaken in him memories of how You have rescued him from danger, saved him from eternal judgment, and protected him from harm in the past. Great is Your faithfulness, O God.

His Eyes

I was blind but now I see! *John 9:25*

Loving Father, open my husband's eyes to see Your handiwork all around. Protect him from spiritual blindness that would prevent him from seeing Your glory in what You have made and all that You do. Help him to remember that once he was blind but You enabled him to see.

His Ears

Tune your ears to wisdom, and concentrate on understanding.

Proverbs 2:2, NLT

Lord, tune my husband's ear to wisdom and understanding. Prompt him to turn away from foolish people and foolish talk and toward wise people and wise words.

His Mouth

He who guards his lips guards his life, but he who speaks rashly will come to ruin. *Proverbs 13:3*

Guard my husband's lips. Make him mindful of what he speaks and when he speaks. Help him to weigh his words wisely before they escape the door of his mouth and to refrain from rash words that he would later regret.

His Neck

Give me understanding, and I will keep your law and obey it with all my heart. *Psalm 119:34*

God of all wisdom, when my husband has to make a decision today, I pray he will weigh his options on the scale of Your Word. Give him understanding so he will know the right path to take and the best choice to make.

His Shoulders

The LORD is my shepherd, I shall not be in want. *Psalm 23:1*

Lord, thank You for being the Great Shepherd who leads, protects, and cares for my husband. Remind him that because You are his Shepherd, he has everything he needs.

His Heart

If I had cherished sin in my heart, the Lord would not have listened; but God has surely listened and heard my voice in prayer. *Psalm 66:18–19*

I pray my husband will not cherish or hold on to any sin in his heart. Convict him to confess his sin quickly and repent from his sin completely. In Jesus' name, amen.

His Back

> Have you not put a hedge around him and his household and everything he has? *Job 1:10*

Almighty Lord, place a hedge of protection around my husband, our household, and everything we have. Surround my husband on all sides with Your protective presence. Preserve his going out and his coming in. Keep him under Your watchful eye and tender care.

His Arms

> Look to the LORD and his strength; seek his face always.
> *1 Chronicles 16:11*

Prompt my husband to look to You and Your strength rather than depend on his own. Whether it is strength to follow Your ways or to turn away from temptation, I pray he will not rely on his own willpower but on Your mighty power.

His Hands

> The LORD will open the heavens, the storehouse of his bounty, to send rain on your land in season and to bless all the work of your hands. You will lend to many nations but will borrow from none. The LORD will make you the head, not the tail. If you pay attention to the commands of the LORD your God that I give you this day and carefully follow them, you will always be at the top, never at the bottom. *Deuteronomy 28:12–13*

Heavenly Father, place a desire and determination in my husband to pay attention to and follow Your commands so that he will always be at the top and never at the bottom, so that he will be the head and not the tail. Please, Lord, open the storehouse of Your bounty and rain down blessings on the work of his hands.

His Ring Finger

Let love and faithfulness never leave you; bind them around your neck, write them on the tablet of your heart. *Proverbs 3:3*

Lord, I pray my husband's love for me and faithfulness to our marriage will never leave his heart. May he bind our vows around his neck and write them on the tablet of his heart. No matter what struggles we may face, I pray his love for me and my love for him will never wane.

His Side

He who walks with the wise grows wise, but a companion of fools suffers harm. *Proverbs 13:20*

Help my husband cultivate friendships with people who are wise and weed out relationships with those who are foolish. Show him how to quickly discern the difference.

His Sexuality

For you created my inmost being; you knit me together in my mother's womb. I praise you because I am fearfully and wonderfully made; your works are wonderful, I know that full well. *Psalm 139:13–14*

Thank You for creating my husband's inmost being, for having knit him together in his mother's womb. I praise You because he is fearfully and wonderfully made; Your works are wonderful, I know that full well. I praise You for the meticulous way You fashioned the sexual aspects of his body. I pray You will bless him with vitality and good health.

His Legs

Elijah went before the people and said, "How long will you waver between two opinions? If the LORD is God, follow him; but if Baal is God, follow him." *1 Kings 18:21*

Strengthen my husband's faith so that he will not waver in what he believes but stand firm in his faith and follow You.

His Knees

> For the eyes of the LORD range throughout the earth to strengthen those whose hearts are fully committed to him. *2 Chronicles 16:9*

Lord, as Your eyes range throughout the earth to strengthen those whose hearts are fully committed to You, I pray they will rest on my husband. Show him what it means to be fully committed to You, and empower him to make that a reality in his life. As he exercises his faith regularly, please increase his strength mightily.

His Feet

> He will guard the feet of his saints, but the wicked will be silenced in darkness. *1 Samuel 2:9*

Blessed Father, guard my husband's feet as he walks the path of life. Guide his every step. Protect him from being lured into darkness, and keep him on the well-lit path of Your perfect will. In Jesus' name, amen.

Day Six

His Mind

Jesus replied: "Love the Lord your God with all your heart and with all your soul and with all your mind." Matthew 22:37

Dear Lord, stir my husband to love You with all his mind. Keep him from falling into the trap of routine religion, and show him how to have an intimate relationship with You. Let his mind be centered on You. May his every thought be sifted through the sieve of Your love for him.

His Eyes

I made a covenant with my eyes not to look lustfully at a girl. Job 31:1

Lord, I am struck with the fact that Job was described as "the finest man in all the earth…a man of complete integrity" (Job 1:8, NLT), and yet he felt the pull to look at women with lust in his eyes. Help my husband see the danger of looking in the wrong direction. Give him the desire to make a covenant with his eyes to not look lustfully at any woman or image of a woman. Empower him to turn his head in the opposite direction when temptation arises.

His Ears

[The Lord] takes the upright into his confidence. Proverbs 3:32

Make my husband a man with whom You can share Your secrets and whom You can take into Your confidence. I pray that he will lean into You and listen carefully as he would listen to a close and trusted friend. In Jesus' name, amen.

His Mouth

Even a fool is thought wise if he keeps silent, and discerning if he holds his tongue. *Proverbs 17:28*

Help my husband hold his tongue when it is in his best interests to do so. Give him the wisdom and discernment to remain silent in any situation in which his words would not be profitable, helpful, or edifying to those listening.

His Neck

Teach me knowledge and good judgment, for I believe in your commands. *Psalm 119:66*

God of all wisdom, teach my husband knowledge and good judgment, so that he will make decisions that honor and glorify You.

His Shoulders

How abundant are the good things that you have stored up for those who fear you, that you bestow in the sight of all, on those who take refuge in you. *Psalm 31:19, NIV 2011*

Remove any worry or anxiety from my husband, and remind him that You have good things stored up for him. Rather than his feeling like he has to carry the weight of the world on his shoulders, help my husband to trust in Your abundant provision available to those who fear Your name.

His Heart

My flesh and my heart may fail, but God is the strength of my heart and my portion forever. *Psalm 73:26*

Even though my husband's physical heart may wear out, his bones may grow brittle, and his skin may sag, I pray You will keep his spiritual heart strong and his soul secure. May he remember that You are the strength of his heart and his portion forever; You are all he needs.

His Back

> But you are a shield around me, O LORD; you bestow glory on me and lift up my head. *Psalm 3:3*

Almighty God, be a shield around my husband, covering him from head to toe, from front to back. Deliver him from evil. Protect him from harm. Lift his head in the confident assurance that You are his Rock, Strong Tower, and Sure Defense.

His Arms

> David also said to Solomon his son, "Be strong and courageous, and do the work. Do not be afraid or discouraged, for the LORD God, my God, is with you." *1 Chronicles 28:20*

As my husband faces the tasks of his day, help him be strong and courageous to do the work You have called him to do. I pray he will not be afraid or discouraged, knowing You are with him to sustain him when he grows weary and to strengthen him when he grows weak.

His Hands

> Do not let this Book of the Law depart from your mouth; meditate on it day and night, so that you may be careful to do everything written in it. Then you will be prosperous and successful. *Joshua 1:8*

I pray my husband will not let Your Word depart from his mouth as he goes about his work today. Prompt him to meditate on Your Word day and night so that he may be careful to do everything written in it. Open his eyes to the correlation between godly living and successful endeavors. May You bless the work of his hands to make him prosperous and successful.

His Ring Finger

Drink water from your own cistern, running water from your own well.
Proverbs 5:15

I pray my husband will be satisfied with the water from his own cistern—that he will be sexually gratified and fulfilled by me alone. Remove all temptation to drink from any well but his own. Make me sensitive to his sexual needs and desires, and help me satisfy him so that he will not leave home thirsty and vulnerable to the Enemy's tempting tactics.

His Side

If your enemy is hungry, give him food to eat; if he is thirsty, give him water to drink. In doing this, you will heap burning coals on his head, and the LORD will reward you. *Proverbs 25:21–22*

If someone is unkind or cruel to my husband today, give him the discipline and determination not to retaliate with anger or malice but to respond with kindness and grace. Give him inner strength and the willpower to respond to those who oppose him with the cool drink of a kind word.

His Sexuality

For the lips of an adulteress drip honey, and her speech is smoother than oil; but in the end she is bitter as gall, sharp as a double-edged sword. Her feet go down to death; her steps lead straight to the grave.
Proverbs 5:3–5

Protect my husband from seductive women. Give him the power to turn away from any woman who tries to entice him, tempt him, or trap him. May he recognize such a woman as bitter gall, a double-edged sword, and destructive bait that would ruin his life. I ask You to place a hedge of protection around him so that such a woman cannot reach in to grab him or even tap him on the shoulder.

His Legs

> You will not have to fight this battle. Take up your positions; stand firm
> and see the deliverance the LORD will give you, O Judah and Jerusalem.
> Do not be afraid; do not be discouraged. Go out to face them tomor-
> row, and the LORD will be with you. *2 Chronicles 20:17*

Almighty God, reassure my husband that he need not fight his battles on
his own. Teach him to stand firm in the knowledge of who he is in Christ.
Help him not be afraid or discouraged but secure and sure. Empower him
to go out and face the day standing firm, knowing that You are with him.

His Knees

> Now when Daniel learned that the decree had been published,
> he went home to his upstairs room where the windows opened
> toward Jerusalem. Three times a day he got down on his knees
> and prayed, giving thanks to his God, just as he had done before.
> *Daniel 6:10*

Fill my husband with the power of the Holy Spirit so that he will not let
anyone or anything prevent him from worshiping You. May he be like
Daniel, who refused to hide his faith even though it was punishable by
death. No matter what pressures are placed on him, let my husband bow
only and always to You, O Lord.

His Feet

> He makes my feet like the feet of a deer, he enables me to go on the
> heights. *Habakkuk 3:19*

Lord, make my husband's feet like the feet of a deer and enable him to
stand surefooted on the rocky heights. Keep him secure and confident on
the mountain trails of difficulty and the rough terrain of trials. In Jesus'
name, amen.

Day Seven

His Mind

He [Satan] was a murderer from the beginning, not holding to the truth, for there is no truth in him. When he lies, he speaks his native language, for he is a liar and the father of lies. *John 8:44*

Dear Lord, protect my husband's mind from the Evil One's influence. Because every spiritual battle is won or lost at the threshold of the mind, I pray that my husband will not answer the door when the Enemy knocks. Help him recognize the Enemy's lies quickly, reject them completely, and replace them with Your truth.

His Eyes

My ears had heard of you but now my eyes have seen you. *Job 42:5*

Open my husband's eyes to recognize You actively working in his life. Help him see manifestations of Your glory and Your presence throughout the day.

His Ears

Blessed is the man who listens to me [wisdom], watching daily at my doors, waiting at my doorway. For whoever finds me finds life and receives favor from the LORD. *Proverbs 8:34–35*

Lord, teach my husband how to listen carefully to wise words. I pray he will rise each morning with eager expectation to grow in wisdom and truth. Help him to be attentive to Your voice, alert to Your instruction, and sensitive to Your gentle whispers. Reveal to him the blessings and favor that come to a man who turns his ears toward You.

His Mouth

A gentle answer turns away wrath, but a harsh word stirs up anger.

Proverbs 15:1

No matter what someone says or does to irritate my husband today, give him the mercy and grace he needs to give a gentle answer in return. Prevent him from responding to harsh words with harsh words, angry words with angry words, or spiteful words with spiteful words. May his words not stoke the fire of anger but instead extinguish the flames of conflict.

His Neck

Teach me to do your will, for you are my God. May your gracious Spirit lead me forward on a firm footing. *Psalm 143:10,* NLT

Teach my husband to do Your will. Show him the best choice for every decision he has to make today. Fill him with the knowledge of Your will so that he will be able to evaluate his options wisely and choose Your best confidently. May Your Holy Spirit lead him forward on the firm footing of right choices.

His Shoulders

I sought the LORD, and he answered me; he delivered me from all my fears. *Psalm 34:4*

When my husband begins to feel the weight of the world on his shoulders, I pray he will seek You, call out to You, and depend on You. Deliver him from all his fears, and teach him to trust in You.

His Heart

Teach me your way, O LORD, and I will walk in your truth; give me an undivided heart, that I may fear your name. *Psalm 86:11*

Teach my husband Your way, that he may walk in Your truth. Give him an undivided heart, that he may fear Your name. Keep him from being wishy-washy when it comes to his faith but decidedly sure and wholly Yours.

His Back

> But let all who take refuge in you be glad; let them ever sing for joy. Spread your protection over them, that those who love your name may rejoice in you. *Psalm 5:11*

Thank You, Lord, that my husband can take refuge in the strong tower of Your love. Spread Your protective canopy over him as a mother hen shelters her chicks under the shadow of her wings. Keep him from harm in both the physical and spiritual realms.

His Arms

> In your hands are strength and power to exalt and give strength to all. *1 Chronicles 29:12*

Lord, please give my husband physical, emotional, and spiritual strength today. Make him a conduit through which Your mighty power flows.

His Hands

> In everything he did he had great success, because the LORD was with him. *1 Samuel 18:14*

I pray my husband will have great success in everything he does today. Help him know that his accomplishments and achievements are because of Your blessing and presence in his life.

His Ring Finger

> May your fountain be blessed, and may you rejoice in the wife of your youth. A loving doe, a graceful deer—may her breasts satisfy

you always, may you ever be captivated by her love.
Proverbs 5:18–19

I pray my husband's fountain will be blessed with vitality and health. Let our lovemaking refresh, renew, and re-energize his entire being. Help me remember the importance of being like a loving doe: gentle and attractive. May he be captivated by my love and be sexually fulfilled by our physical intimacy.

His Side

A friend loves at all times. *Proverbs 17:17*

Teach my husband what it means to be a friend who loves at all times, especially when a friend is hard to love. And, Lord, please bless him with a friend who will do the same for him.

His Sexuality

Flee from sexual immorality. All other sins a man commits are outside his body, but he who sins sexually sins against his own body. Do you not know that your body is a temple of the Holy Spirit, who is in you, whom you have received from God? You are not your own; you were bought at a price. Therefore honor God with your body. *1 Corinthians 6:18–20*

Lord, help my husband flee from sexual immorality with the speed of an Olympic sprinter. Remind him that his body is the temple of the Holy Spirit, and empower him to keep it holy, healthy, and sexually pure. I pray he will remember that he is not his own but that he has been purchased by the precious blood of Jesus Christ.

His Legs

I have set the LORD always before me. Because he is at my right hand, I will not be shaken. *Psalm 16:8*

I pray my husband will keep You at the center of his life. Help him stand firm in the truth and not be shaken by the shifting values of our culture. Don't let him falter in his faith or cower in fear; rather, let him meet every situation with full confidence that You are at his right hand to sustain him and support him.

His Knees

Come, let us bow down in worship, let us kneel before the LORD our Maker; for he is our God and we are the people of his pasture, the flock under his care. *Psalm 95:6–7*

Stir my husband to bend his knee in humble submission to You and awe-inspired worship of You. May he pause often to praise You for who You are and thank You for what You do.

His Feet

You have made known to me the path of life; you will fill me with joy in your presence, with eternal pleasures at your right hand. *Psalm 16:11*

I pray You will show my husband the road map to the abundant, victorious life in Christ. Fill him with joy and peace as he walks in constant communion and unbroken union with You. Allow him to experience eternal pleasures in the joy of Your presence as he grabs hold of Your right hand. In Jesus' name, amen.

Day Eight

His Mind

The thief [Satan] comes only to steal and kill and destroy; I [Jesus] have come that they may have life, and have it to the full. *John 10:10*

Heavenly Father, protect my husband's mind against the lies of the Enemy, who seeks to steal, kill, and destroy. Place a wall of protection around my husband's thought life to keep out thoughts that lead to discouragement, discontentment, and destruction. Usher in thoughts that lead to the abundant life Jesus came to give—life to the full.

His Eyes

The precepts of the LORD are right, giving joy to the heart. The commands of the LORD are radiant, giving light to the eyes.
Psalm 19:8

May Your Holy Spirit give light to my husband's eyes so that he will be able to see clearly the difference between right and wrong, holy and sinful, the truth and a lie. Give him radiant joy as he keeps Your precepts and commands as the guiding principles of his life.

His Ears

Listen to my [wisdom's] instruction and be wise; do not ignore it. Blessed is the man who listens to me, watching daily at my doors, waiting at my doorway. For whoever finds me finds life and receives favor from the LORD. *Proverbs 8:33–35*

Open my husband's ears to wise instruction so that he can be wise. Help him pay attention to godly counsel and not ignore it. May he find favor with You as he walks the road paved with the wise words of others.

His Mouth

> The tongue that brings healing is a tree of life, but a deceitful tongue crushes the spirit. *Proverbs 15:4*

Show my husband ways that he can use his words to bring healing and joy into the lives of others. Keep him from saying anything that would crush someone's spirit, discourage someone's dreams, or tear down someone's character.

His Neck

> The fear of the LORD is the beginning of knowledge, but fools despise wisdom and discipline. *Proverbs 1:7*

May my husband make decisions based on his reverent fear and humble respect of Your sovereignty and holiness. Stir up a desire in him to seek Your wisdom for every decision and Your direction for every choice. I pray he will not depend on worldly knowledge with its human limitations but on Your infinite wisdom, which knows no bounds.

His Shoulders

> The lions may grow weak and hungry, but those who seek the LORD lack no good thing. *Psalm 34:10*

Thank You for the promise that those who seek You lack no good thing. I pray my husband will not carry the unnecessary burden of trying to meet all of his and our family's needs on his own but trust in Your promised provision and care.

His Heart

> I have hidden your word in my heart that I might not sin against you. *Psalm 119:11*

Put a hunger in my husband's heart to meditate on Your Word. Hide Your Word in his heart—let it sink into the core of his being—so that he will not sin against You.

His Back

> Show me the wonders of your great love, you who save by your
> right hand those who take refuge in you from their foes. Keep
> me as the apple of your eye; hide me in the shadow of your wings.
> *Psalm 17:7–8,* NIV 2011

Almighty God, show my husband the wonder of Your great love, and deliver him by the power of Your right hand. Protect him from his foes, and draw him into Your safe place of refuge. Lord, keep him as the apple of Your eye, and hide him in the shadow of Your wings.

His Arms

> But as for you, be strong and do not give up, for your work will be
> rewarded. *2 Chronicles 15:7*

Strengthen my husband so that he will not give up, grow weary, or get discouraged. I ask that You equip, energize, and encourage him with the power of the Holy Spirit. Please reward him with blessings outpoured as he completes the work You have called him to do.

His Hands

> He [Uzziah] sought God during the days of Zechariah, who instructed
> him in the fear of God. As long as he sought the LORD, God gave him
> success. *2 Chronicles 26:5*

I pray my husband will seek You with all his heart, not only to obtain financial success but also in order to serve You and honor You. Please help him see his work as a way of glorifying You and representing You in the world. Lord, bless the works of his hands today.

His Ring Finger

Her husband has full confidence in her and lacks nothing of value. She brings him good, not harm, all the days of her life. *Proverbs 31:11–12*

Lord, I pray that my husband will have full confidence and complete trust in me. Show me how to meet his needs and do him good so that he will lack nothing of value. Help my attitude toward him not be dependent on his actions as a husband but on my commitment to love him as You have called me to.

His Side

As iron sharpens iron, so one man sharpens another. *Proverbs 27:17*

Please bless my husband with a friend who sharpens him—one who challenges him, inspires him, and holds him accountable. Give him wisdom and grace to do the same for the close friends in his life.

His Sexuality

The body is not meant for sexual immorality, but for the Lord, and the Lord for the body. *1 Corinthians 6:13*

Thank You for the gift of sexual intimacy in marriage. Keep my husband from abusing this gift in any way, and help him maintain high moral principles and honorable practices.

His Legs

Some trust in chariots and some in horses, but we trust in the name of the LORD our God. They are brought to their knees and fall, but we rise up and stand firm. *Psalm 20:7–8*

Lord God, I pray my husband will not put his trust in people, power, or possessions but in You alone. When those around him buckle under the world's pressure to conform to ungodly principles and unholy practices, bolster my husband to rise up and stand firm in Your truth.

His Knees

> If my people, who are called by my name, will humble themselves and pray and seek my face and turn from their wicked ways, then will I hear from heaven and will forgive their sin and will heal their land.
> *2 Chronicles 7:14*

Move my husband to humble himself before You today, to pray and seek Your face. Prompt him to turn from any sinful way in his life, knowing that You will forgive him completely and restore him fully.

His Feet

> My steps have held to your paths; my feet have not slipped. *Psalm 17:5*

Keep my husband's feet steadily moving on Your paths so he does not deviate from Your plan. Guide his steps so that he will not slip on seductive sin but walk surefooted in righteous conviction. In Jesus' name, amen.

Day Nine

His Mind

> Those who live according to the sinful nature have their minds set on what that nature desires; but those who live in accordance with the Spirit have their minds set on what the Spirit desires.
> *Romans 8:5*

Dear Lord, please help my husband set his mind on what the Spirit desires today: love, joy, peace, patience, kindness, goodness, faithfulness, gentleness, and self-control. When the desires of the flesh try to weasel their way into my husband's mind, give him discernment to recognize them quickly and reject the thoughts completely.

His Eyes

> I am still confident of this: I will see the goodness of the LORD in the land of the living. *Psalm 27:13*

Open my husband's eyes to recognize Your goodness throughout his day. Instead of his being so distracted by the busyness of the day that he misses Your holy Post-it notes, help him heed Your prompts to "turn aside" as Moses did so that he can see the burning bushes in his own backyard (Exodus 3:4, NASB). Let him see You in moments of sudden glory where You make Your presence known.

His Ears

> The way of fools seems right to them, but the wise listen to advice.
> *Proverbs 12:15*, NIV 2011

Open my husband's ears to listen to wise advice and instruction. Make his inner man sensitive to the promptings of the Holy Spirit.

His Mouth

The heart of the righteous weighs its answers, but the mouth of the wicked gushes evil. *Proverbs 15:28*

Help my husband weigh his answers before he speaks and not say the first words that come to his mind. Let his words resonate with righteousness and carry not even a hint of evil, anger, bitterness, pride, or contempt.

His Neck

For the LORD gives wisdom, and from his mouth come knowledge and understanding. *Proverbs 2:6*

Father, give my husband the wisdom, knowledge, and understanding he needs to make godly decisions. Keep the world, the flesh, or the devil from turning his head so he can make decisions that honor You.

His Shoulders

Why are you downcast, O my soul? Why so disturbed within me? Put your hope in God, for I will yet praise him, my Savior and my God. *Psalm 42:5–6*

When my husband begins to feel the weight of daily burdens, I pray You will remind him that You are the Burden-Bearer. Help him put his hope in You! When he feels all tied up in knots, Lord, please loosen the cords of worry with the fingers of praise.

His Heart

My heart is set on keeping your decrees to the very end. *Psalm 119:112*

I pray my husband's heart will be set on keeping Your decrees until he takes his last breath. Please don't let anything lure his heart away from following and loving You.

His Back

> The LORD is my rock, my fortress and my deliverer;
> my God is my rock, in whom I take refuge. He is my
> shield and the horn of my salvation, my stronghold.
>
> *Psalm 18:2*

Thank You, Lord, for being my husband's Rock, Fortress, and Deliverer in whom he can take refuge. Shield him from harm. Protect him from evil. Just as an animal's horn is a symbol of strength and a means of protection, I pray You will be the horn of my husband's salvation—his strength, his protection, and his stronghold of safety. Thank You, Lord, for having my husband's back today.

His Arms

> Nehemiah said,..."Do not grieve, for the joy of the LORD is your
> strength." *Nehemiah 8:10*

I pray that the joy of Your presence, O Lord, will be my husband's strength today. Rather than his focusing on his weakness, remind him that he has the power of the Holy Spirit living in him and working through him.

His Hands

> In everything that he [Hezekiah] undertook in the service of
> God's temple and in obedience to the law and the commands,
> he sought his God and worked wholeheartedly. And so he
> prospered. *2 Chronicles 31:21*

Help my husband to view his work as serving You rather than serving man. Stir his heart to work wholeheartedly to glorify You in all he does. May he praise You for all the ways You cause him to prosper.

His Ring Finger

> Ah, Sovereign LORD, you have made the heavens and the earth by
> your great power and outstretched arm. Nothing is too hard for you.
> *Jeremiah 32:17*

Lord, shape our marriage into a beautiful representation of Christ and the Church. Even though we are far from perfect, I know nothing is too hard for You. Please make my man the husband You've purposed him to be, and make me the wife You've purposed me to be. Help us both to be malleable in Your hands. Oh Lord, I believe in miracles. Nothing is too hard for You.

His Side

> And let us consider how we may spur one another on toward love and
> good deeds. *Hebrews 10:24*

Loving Lord, inspire my husband to think of ways to motivate his friends, family, and coworkers toward acts of love and good deeds. Prompt him to foster spiritual growth and compassionate acts in the lives of those with whom he walks side by side.

His Sexuality

> His mouth is sweetness itself; he is altogether lovely. This is my lover,
> this my friend. *Song of Songs 5:16*

Help me respond to my husband in such a way that he will know his kisses are sweetness itself. Show me ways that I can assure him that I am attracted to him and pleased by him. I pray he will be secure in the knowledge that he is my lover and my friend and that he will feel fulfilled in our sexual relationship. Keep me from allowing our intimacy to wane in complacency, and show me how to fan the flame of passion.

His Legs

My feet stand on level ground; in the great assembly I will praise the
LORD. *Psalm 26:12*

I pray my husband will stand firm on the level ground of Your truth
and not wobble on the shifting sand of the culture that changes
what is right and wrong, true and false, fact and fiction on any given
day.

His Knees

To the faithful you show yourself faithful, to the blameless
you show yourself blameless, to the pure you show yourself
pure, but to the crooked you show yourself shrewd. You save
the humble but bring low those whose eyes are haughty. *Psalm
18:25–27*

Strengthen my husband's resolve to be faithful to You so that You will
show Yourself faithful, to be blameless so that You will show Yourself
blameless, and to be pure so that You will show Yourself pure. Block
any tendency in his heart to be proud or arrogant. Show him how to
live in humility and submission like a war horse under the control of its
master.

His Feet

Even though I walk through the valley of the shadow of death, I will
fear no evil, for you are with me; your rod and your staff, they comfort
me. *Psalm 23:4*

Even if my husband has to walk through the darkest valley, the most
difficult circumstance, or even a life-threatening situation, I pray he
will not be afraid of evil or the perilous schemes of the devil. Blan-

ket him in the peace of knowing that You are with him every step of the way. Prod him forward with Your rod when he lags behind, and pull him back with Your staff when he runs ahead. In Jesus' name, amen.

Day Ten

His Mind

> The mind of sinful man is death, but the mind controlled by the Spirit is
> life and peace. *Romans 8:6*

I pray my husband's mind will not be governed by the flesh, which seeks
to meet his needs apart from Christ. Instead let him be controlled by the
Holy Spirit living in him and working through him. When any sinful
thoughts come into his mind, help him reject them quickly and completely so that he can live in peace.

His Eyes

> Turn my eyes away from worthless things; preserve my life according
> to your word. *Psalm 119:37*

Today I ask You to prompt my husband to turn his eyes away from worth-
less things that catch his attention. Preserve his life and his integrity by
helping him divert his eyes from anything or anyone that would cause
him to stumble—mentally, physically, or spiritually.

His Ears

> Ears that hear and eyes that see—
> the LORD has made them both.
> *Proverbs 20:12*

Loving Father, open my husband's ears to hear You and his eyes to
see You. Help him to detect the gentle whisper of Your voice in his
inner man. May he know at day's end that You have spoken to him
today.

His Mouth

Death and life are in the power of the tongue. *Proverbs 18:21,* NASB

I pray my husband will use his words to speak life and not death to those around him. Guard his tongue so that his words will build up and not tear down, encourage and not discourage, heal and not hurt.

His Neck

Discretion will protect you, and understanding will guard you. Wisdom will save you from the ways of wicked men, from men whose words are perverse, who leave the straight paths to walk in dark ways. *Proverbs 2:11–13*

Lord, instruct my husband in how to be a man who shows discretion and understanding. Protect him from making bad decisions, and lead him to choose Your best.

His Shoulders

Praise be to the Lord, to God our Savior, who daily bears our burdens. *Psalm 68:19*

Lord, I praise You for carrying our burdens every day. Thank You for never getting tired of them or weary under them. I pray my husband will release his burdens and place them on Your able shoulders—today and every day.

His Heart

The heart is deceitful above all things. *Jeremiah 17:9*

While the world says, "Follow your heart; do what *feels* right," Your Word tells us the heart cannot be trusted; it is deceitful above all things. I pray my husband will not rely on his feelings but sift every decision through the sieve of truth.

His Back

> The wicked lie in wait for the righteous, seeking their very lives;
> but the LORD will not leave them in their power or let them be
> condemned when brought to trial. *Psalm 37:32–33*

Protect my husband from wicked people who look for opportunities to bring him down or trip him up. Deliver him from the power of those who would set out to harm him, and foil their attempts to mar his good name. Help him rest in the assurance of Your divine protection and intercession.

His Arms

> David found strength in the LORD his God. *1 Samuel 30:6*

When my husband is discouraged, help him find strength in You, O Lord our God. I pray he will not depend on people, possessions, or position to lift his spirits but that he will find encouragement in You.

His Hands

> [Nehemiah prayed,] "O Lord, let your ear be attentive to the prayer of
> this your servant and to the prayer of your servants who delight in
> revering your name. Give your servant success today by granting him
> favor in the presence of this man." *Nehemiah 1:11*

Just as Nehemiah prayed for a favorable response before he made his request to the king, prompt my husband to pray to receive favor before he makes presentations or requests to others in his field of business. Give him wisdom, courage, and strength to go about his work with confidence, knowing that You are with him.

His Ring Finger

"For I hate divorce!" says the LORD, the God of Israel. "To divorce your wife is to overwhelm her with cruelty," says the LORD of Heaven's Armies. "So guard your heart; do not be unfaithful to your wife." *Malachi 2:16,* NLT

Loving Father, prevent the word *divorce* from entering our marriage vocabulary. I know You hate divorce—the violent dismembering of the "one flesh" of marriage. I pray we will both be on guard to protect our marriage vows. Give us the power of the Holy Spirit to work through difficulties. Help us not to tear apart what You have joined together.

His Side

Though one may be overpowered, two can defend themselves. A cord of three strands is not quickly broken. *Ecclesiastes 4:12*

Give my husband a good friend who will stick with him through thick and thin. May he have a godly ally with whom he can form a three-stranded bond: my husband, his friend, and Jesus. Strengthen this strand of three into an unbreakable alliance to withstand the stress and strain of life.

His Sexuality

I belong to my lover, and his desire is for me. *Song of Songs 7:10*

I pray my husband will desire me and only me. Protect his eyes from straying, his heart from lusting, and his mind from ungodly imaginings.

His Legs

He lifted me out of the slimy pit, out of the mud and mire; he set my feet on a rock and gave me a firm place to stand. *Psalm 40:2*

When my husband feels as if he is sinking in despair, discouragement, or depression, I pray You will lift him out of the slimy pit and set his feet on the solid rock of Jesus Christ. Keep him from wobbling in weakness, and strengthen him to stand firm in his faith.

His Knees

> Now I, Nebuchadnezzar, praise and exalt and glorify the King of heaven, because everything he does is right and all his ways are just. And those who walk in pride he is able to humble. *Daniel 4:37*

Stir my husband's heart to exalt You as Sovereign King of heaven. Help him to trust in the truth that everything You do is right and all Your ways are just. Keep him from walking in pride, and cause him to kneel before You in humble submission. I pray You will not have to bring him to his knees through trials and troubles, but that he will willingly bow in worship and adoration of Your righteous reign in his life.

His Feet

> He will not let your foot slip—he who watches over you will not slumber; indeed, he who watches over Israel will neither slumber nor sleep. *Psalm 121:3–4*

Lord, what a comfort to know that You never slumber; indeed, You who watch over my husband will neither slumber nor sleep. I pray You will not let my husband's foot slip—that he will not stumble on the rocks of temptation or fall into the ditches of sin. Open his eyes to detect the precisely positioned snares of Satan intended to trip him up and bring him down. In Jesus' name, amen.

Day Eleven

His Mind

The sinful mind is hostile to God. It does not submit to God's law, nor can it do so. *Romans 8:7*

Heavenly Father, may my husband's mind be at peace with You today. I pray he will not be hostile toward You in any way—that he will not reject Your commands but embrace them, that he will not turn away from Your love but bask in it, that he will not resist Your authority but willingly submit to it.

His Eyes

Then God opened her eyes and she saw a well of water. So she went and filled the skin with water and gave the boy a drink. *Genesis 21:19*

Just as You opened Hagar's eyes to see the well that had been there all along, I ask that You will open my husband's eyes to see the many ways You have provided for his needs. Please don't let him miss seeing Your blessings today.

His Ears

He who answers before listening—
that is his folly and his shame. *Proverbs 18:13*

Lord, help my husband listen carefully before he gives a reply. Protect him from being put to shame for speaking too quickly; instead, let him be seen as wise for listening intently.

His Mouth

> He who loves a pure heart and whose speech is gracious will have the king for his friend. *Proverbs 22:11*

Father, I pray my husband's speech will be seasoned with grace, as if every word were a gift to the hearer. May he find favor with leaders and those in authority over him because of the grace and wisdom of his words.

His Neck

> Trust in the LORD with all your heart and lean not on your own understanding; in all your ways acknowledge him, and he will make your paths straight. *Proverbs 3:5–6*

Teach my husband to trust in You with all his heart and not lean on his own understanding. Stir him to rely on Your direction rather than depending on his own reasoning. May he acknowledge You in every decision he has to make today, taking great care to please You and glorify You in all he does. Please remove any confusion that clouds his thinking, and lift any fog that makes Your way difficult to see.

His Shoulders

> As pressure and stress bear down on me, I find joy in your commands. *Psalm 119:143*, NLT

When my husband feels the strain of life bearing down on him, remind him to trust in You. May he remember that Your commands are not to make life harder but to make life easier. Help him find joy in Your commands that instruct him on how to live life to the full.

His Heart

> Let not my heart be drawn to what is evil, to take part in wicked deeds with men who are evildoers; let me not eat of their delicacies. *Psalm 141:4*

Shield my husband's heart from being drawn toward the deeds of evil-doers and wicked men, and lead him toward good works and godly men. Shield him from envying the enticing delicacies of sin, and encourage him to feast on the fruit of a pure heart and godly living.

His Back

> [Jesus prayed,] "Holy Father, protect them by the power of your name—the name you gave me—so that they may be one as we are one." *John 17:11*

Just as Jesus asked that You protect His friends by the power of Your name, I ask that You protect my husband by the power of Your name. May he be one with You today and every day.

His Arms

> Wait for the LORD; be strong and take heart and wait for the LORD. *Psalm 27:14*

Help my husband wait for You, rather than run ahead of You today. Strengthen his faith and encourage his heart by the power of the Holy Spirit.

His Hands

> May the favor of the Lord our God rest upon us; establish the work of our hands for us—yes, establish the work of our hands. *Psalm 90:17*

May Your favor rest upon my husband today, Lord God. Establish the work of his hands and give him great success.

His Ring Finger

> A new command I [Jesus] give you: Love one another. As I have loved you, so you must love one another. *John 13:34*

I pray my husband and I will love each other in the same way that Your Son, Jesus, has loved us—sacrificially, completely, and unconditionally.

His Side

> Do not judge, or you too will be judged. For in the same way you judge others, you will be judged, and with the measure you use, it will be measured to you.... First take the plank out of your own eye, and then you will see clearly to remove the speck from your brother's eye.
> *Matthew 7:1–2, 5*

Help my husband resist the temptation to judge, criticize, or condemn others so that he will not be judged, criticized, or condemned. Make him aware of the plank in his own eye before he attempts to take the speck from his brother's eye. Rather than point out the weaknesses and faults of others, lead him to work on correcting his own faults and strengthening his own weaknesses.

His Sexuality

> Many waters cannot quench love; rivers cannot wash it away.
> *Song of Songs 8:7*

I pray nothing will quench my husband's desire for me. I pray You will prevent any dams from obstructing the flow, any drought from diminishing the flow, or any obstacle from diverting the flow of love in our marriage.

His Legs

> He alone is my rock and my salvation; he is my fortress, I will not be shaken. *Psalm 62:6*

Lord, our Rock and our Salvation, help my husband stand firm in his faith and strong in his convictions. I pray he will not be shot down by others, shaken up by circumstances, or shut down by the schemes of the Enemy. Strengthen his resolve so that he will not be moved.

His Knees

The Pharisee stood up and prayed about himself: "God, I thank you that I am not like other men—robbers, evildoers, adulterers—or even like this tax collector. I fast twice a week and give a tenth of all I get." But the tax collector stood at a distance. He would not even look up to heaven, but beat his breast and said, "God, have mercy on me, a sinner." *Luke 18:11–13*

I pray my husband will not be arrogant or proud like the Pharisee who thanked God that he was not as bad as other people, but humble like the tax collector who sought Your mercy, grace, and forgiveness. Keep him from exalting himself so that he will not need to be humbled by You.

His Feet

If the LORD delights in a man's way, he makes his steps firm; though he stumble, he will not fall, for the LORD upholds him with his hand.
Psalm 37:23–24

Lead my husband to walk in a way that delights You. Make his steps firm with faithful conviction. If he stumbles, please catch him with Your hand, Lord, and keep him from falling. In Jesus' name, amen.

Day Twelve

His Mind

Do not conform any longer to the pattern of this world, but be transformed by the renewing of your mind. *Romans 12:2*

I pray my husband will not be conformed to the pattern of this world but be transformed by the renewing of his mind with the Truth. Weed out any thoughts that do not line up with Your Word, and plant new thoughts that will help him grow into the spiritually mature man You created him to be.

His Eyes

Let your eyes look straight ahead, fix your gaze directly before you. *Proverbs 4:25*

Don't let my husband be distracted by the seeming success or prosperity of others. Help him fix his eyes straight ahead on what You have called him to be and to do. Enable him to focus solely on the path You have mapped out for him.

His Ears

The heart of the discerning acquires knowledge; the ears of the wise seek it out. *Proverbs 18:15*

Open my husband's ears to godly advice. Help him tune in to wise words and pay attention to godly wisdom. Make him discerning in what he listens to and cautious about what he allows to enter his mind through his ears.

His Mouth

[There is] a time to be silent and a time to speak. *Ecclesiastes 3:7*

Give my husband wisdom to know when he should be silent and when he should speak up. Grant him discernment to know when to open his mouth and when to keep it closed.

His Neck

> Blessed are those who find wisdom, those who gain understanding, for she is more profitable than silver and yields better returns than gold. She is more precious than rubies; nothing you desire can compare with her. *Proverbs 3:13–15, NIV 2011*

Fill my husband with wisdom and understanding so that he can make the best decisions possible. Show him that making decisions that honor You and bring blessings in the long run is more important than self-seeking decisions that bring financial gain or immediate gratification in the short run. Cultivate in him a desire for Your wisdom over earthly treasures.

His Shoulders

> So do not fear, for I am with you; do not be dismayed, for I am your God. I will strengthen you and help you; I will uphold you with my righteous right hand.... For I am the LORD, your God, who takes hold of your right hand and says to you, Do not fear; I will help you. *Isaiah 41:10, 13*

Protect my husband from being worried about or afraid of the future, and teach him how to rest in the knowledge that You have everything under control. Assure him that You can handle every difficulty that comes his way. Strengthen him and uphold him, for You are the Lord his God who takes hold of his right hand.

His Heart

> Above all else, guard your heart, for it is the wellspring of life.
> *Proverbs 4:23*

Guard my husband's heart against any temptation that comes his way today. Prompt him to keep watch over it with the vigilance of a night watchman patrolling the city walls. Yes, Lord, I pray he will guard his heart, for everything he does and all that he is flows from it.

His Back

> The LORD is my light and my salvation—whom shall I fear? The LORD is the stronghold of my life—of whom shall I be afraid? *Psalm 27:1*

Assure my husband that he has nothing to fear because You are his Light to guide him and his Salvation to sustain him. Help him conquer any fear with the certainty that You are greater than any spiritual or physical foe that would seek to do him harm. Thank You for being the mighty Stronghold of his life.

His Arms

> The LORD is my strength and my shield; my heart trusts in him, and I am helped. My heart leaps for joy and I will give thanks to him in song. *Psalm 28:7*

Heavenly Father, thank You for being my husband's immeasurable Strength and impenetrable Shield. No matter what he has to face today, remind him to trust You fully and confidently. May he jump for joy with songs of praise even before he sees the victory, knowing that it will come.

His Hands

> LORD, grant us success! *Psalm 118:25,* NIV 2011

Lord, grant my husband success! Cause him to flourish in his talents, to thrive in his gifts, and to prosper in his abilities—all of which come from You. Lord, grant him success in his place of employment.

His Ring Finger

To the married I give this command (not I, but the Lord): A wife must not separate from her husband. But if she does, she must remain unmarried or else be reconciled to her husband. And a husband must not divorce his wife. *1 Corinthians 7:10–11*

I pray divorce will not ever be an option in our marriage. No matter how difficult the circumstances, how tumultuous the storm, or how dry the desert, help us keep our commitment to stay true to the vows we made to You and to each other.

His Side

So in everything, do to others what you would have them do to you, for this sums up the Law and the Prophets. *Matthew 7:12*

Loving Lord, help my husband treat others the way that he would like to be treated—with love, honor, and respect.

His Sexuality

You have heard that it was said, "Do not commit adultery." But I tell you that anyone who looks at a woman lustfully has already committed adultery with her in his heart. If your right eye causes you to sin, gouge it out and throw it away. *Matthew 5:27–29*

I pray my husband will not look lustfully at a woman or the image of a woman and thus commit adultery in his heart. Empower him to remove himself from any tempting situation, person, or image, and help him to pluck the temptation right out of his life.

His Legs

In my integrity you uphold me and set me in your presence forever. *Psalm 41:12*

Sovereign Lord, help my husband stand with integrity. I pray his yes will be yes and his no be no. Let him be known as a man who stands on high moral principles and godly character—a man who does what he says he will do.

His Knees

Yet a time is coming and has now come when the true worshipers will worship the Father in spirit and truth, for they are the kind of worshipers the Father seeks. God is spirit, and his worshipers must worship in spirit and in truth. *John 4:23–24*

Keep my husband from getting caught up in empty religious practices and traditions of men that have nothing to do with true worship. Mature and grow his faith to be a continually deepening, personally intimate relationship with You.

His Feet

Praise our God, O peoples, let the sound of his praise be heard; he has preserved our lives and kept our feet from slipping. *Psalm 66:8–9*

I pray You will keep my husband's feet from slipping and make his steps secure. Put a song on his lips and praise in his heart as he lives and moves and has his being in You today. In Jesus' name, amen.

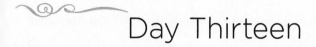

Day Thirteen

His Mind

> Rather, clothe yourselves with the Lord Jesus Christ, and do
> not think about how to gratify the desires of the sinful nature.
> *Romans 13:14*

Heavenly Father, I pray my husband will clothe himself from top to bottom with the Lord Jesus today. Keep him from thinking about ways to gratify the desires of the old sinful nature, and guide him to think about ways to glorify You in all regards.

His Eyes

> Do not lust in your heart after her beauty or let her [the immoral
> woman] captivate you with her eyes. *Proverbs 6:25*

Give my husband the wisdom and the willpower to divert his eyes away from any woman or image of a woman that would captivate his attention or cause him to lust in his heart.

His Ears

> Pay attention and turn your ear to the sayings of the wise;
> apply your heart to what I teach, for it is pleasing when you
> keep them in your heart and have all of them ready on your lips.
> *Proverbs 22:17–18,* NIV 2011

I pray that my husband will pay attention to what he is listening to today. Turn his ears away from the words and songs of fools and toward the words and songs of the wise. Don't let his ears be a conduit through which offensive words infiltrate his mind and thus affect his heart; instead, let him seek out what is pleasing to You and edifying to his soul.

His Mouth

Words from a wise man's mouth are gracious, but a fool is consumed by his own lips. *Ecclesiastes 10:12*

Teach my husband to speak words that are wise and gracious. Keep his conversation free of destructive words that he will later regret, and fill his mouth with gracious words that bring honor and blessing.

His Neck

He who gets wisdom loves his own soul; he who cherishes understanding prospers. *Proverbs 19:8*

Give my husband a desire to seek Your wisdom and understanding for every decision he makes today. Guide him to turn his head on the axis of Your wisdom, plotting his course on the longitude and latitude of Truth, where the truly prosperous life is found.

His Shoulders

I have cared for you since you were born. Yes, I carried you before you were born. I will be your God throughout your lifetime—until your hair is white with age. I made you, and I will care for you. I will carry you along and save you. *Isaiah 46:3–4*, NLT

When my husband is tempted to worry about getting old, help him trust that You will take care of him then, just as You have taken care of him in the past and are taking care of him now. I pray he will remember that You are His Burden-Bearer now and will continue to be when he is old and gray.

His Heart

> A heart at peace gives life to the body, but envy rots the bones.
>
> *Proverbs 14:30*

Instruct my husband in how to have a peaceful heart that ushers in a healthy mind, a strong body, and stable emotions rather than a stress-filled heart that subjects him to a host of physical, emotional, and mental ills. I pray he will not allow envy to creep into his heart but will praise You for all the wonderful ways You provide for his needs.

His Back

> You are my hiding place; you will protect me from trouble and surround me with songs of deliverance. *Psalm 32:7*

Father, protect my husband from trouble today, and surround him with songs of deliverance. When he is afraid, prompt him to rest in You, his hiding place of peace.

His Arms

> My flesh and my heart may fail, but God is the strength of my heart and my portion forever. *Psalm 73:26*

Even when my husband's muscles slacken, his heart slows, and his bones grow brittle, help him remember that You, O God, are his Rock, his firm and faithful Strength. You are his Portion—all he needs on this earth and in the life to come. Keep him strong emotionally and spiritually as he grows old physically.

His Hands

> Blessed are all who fear the LORD, who walk in his ways. You will eat the fruit of your labor; blessings and prosperity will be yours.
>
> *Psalm 128:1–2*

Gracious Lord, please bless the work of my husband's hands and prosper the efforts of his labor. May he enjoy the bountiful harvest of all his hard work.

His Ring Finger

> So, if you think you are standing firm, be careful that you don't fall!
>
> *1 Corinthians 10:12*

I pray neither my husband nor I will be so confident in our marriage that we let our guard down and get lazy. Place a hedge of protection around our marriage to keep the Enemy out and the Holy Spirit in. Don't allow me to grow lax in my efforts to please my husband, but inspire me to work to keep our marriage exciting. Remind him to put a lock on the gate of our love, so that no harmful influences can sneak in unawares. Keep us alert and careful so that we do not fall.

His Side

> If your brother sins against you, go and show him his fault, just between the two of you. If he listens to you, you have won your brother over. *Matthew 18:15*

If someone offends or sins against my husband today, I pray he will not discuss the matter with others but go to the offender directly and settle the issue quickly. Help him resist the temptation to stir up contention or involve others in the offense. Fill him with mercy, wisdom, and grace as he confronts the brother or sister one on one, and let the matter be settled quickly and peacefully.

His Sexuality

> And lead us not into temptation, but deliver us from the evil one.
>
> *Matthew 6:13*

Lead my husband away from temptation and deliver him from the Evil One's enticing traps. Help him see and take the way of escape that You have promised to provide, and protect him from any inclination to look back.

His Legs

If you do not stand firm in your faith, you will not stand at all.
Isaiah 7:9

Help my husband stand firm in his faith and not be swayed by the world's ways. Remind him that if he does not stand steadfast in the truth, he will not stand at all.

His Knees

[Jesus said,] "I am the vine; you are the branches. If a man remains in me and I in him, he will bear much fruit; apart from me you can do nothing." *John 15:5*

Show my husband how to experience constant communion and unbroken union with You. Prevent him from proudly attempting to accomplish anything in his own strength or by his own means, but keep him humbly realizing that apart from You he can accomplish nothing of eternal value or lasting significance. May he stay connected to You, the Vine, so that he can bear much fruit.

His Feet

I will walk about in freedom, for I have sought out your precepts.
Psalm 119:45

Heavenly Father, today help my husband walk about in the freedom that is his in Jesus Christ. I pray that he will not shuffle around in bondage to his past sins or to shame's shackles but that he will stride surefooted with the confidence of a prisoner set free. It is for freedom that Christ has set him free. Hallelujah! (Galatians 5:1). In Jesus' name, amen.

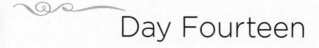

Day Fourteen

His Mind

> For though we live in the world, we do not wage war as the world
> does. The weapons we fight with are not the weapons of the world.
> On the contrary, they have divine power to demolish strongholds. We
> demolish arguments and every pretension that sets itself up against
> the knowledge of God, and we take captive every thought to make it
> obedient to Christ. *2 Corinthians 10:3–5*

Dear Lord, even though we live in a world filled with faulty thinking and pervasive lies, I pray my husband will not buy into what the culture is selling. Empower him to use every spiritual weapon You have given him to fight against the lies of the culture. I pray my husband will take captive every misguided idea of human reasoning, every false argument denouncing Christ, and every rebellious thought contrary to the Word of God. May his every thought be obedient to Christ and His teaching.

His Eyes

> A discerning man keeps wisdom in view, but a fool's eyes wander to
> the ends of the earth. *Proverbs 17:24*

Lord, don't let my husband's eyes be captured by the materialistic trappings of this world. Keep discontentment from entering his heart through what he sees. May shiny cars, bigger homes, finer clothes, or any other temporal toys of the culture not lure his eyes and stir up dissatisfaction with what he has. Help him to keep wisdom in view.

His Ears

> It is better to heed a wise man's rebuke than to listen to the song
> of fools. *Ecclesiastes 7:5*

I pray my husband will be careful about the music he listens to today, not allowing the songs of fools to enter his mind through his ears. Make him sensitive to and aware of any lyrics that are contrary to Christian living. If a song comes on the radio that would affect his soul in a negative way, prompt him to turn it off or change the station.

His Mouth

The Sovereign LORD has given me a well-instructed tongue, to know the word that sustains the weary. *Isaiah 50:4,* NIV 2011

Sovereign Lord, please give my husband a well-instructed tongue. Help him know just the right words to say to someone who is discouraged. Use his words to give strength to the weary, freedom to the captive, healing to the soul-sick friend.

His Neck

The Spirit of the LORD will rest on him—the Spirit of wisdom and of understanding, the Spirit of counsel and of power, the Spirit of knowledge and of the fear of the LORD. *Isaiah 11:2*

Lord, I ask that Your Spirit will rest on my husband today—the Spirit of wisdom and of understanding, the Spirit of counsel and of power, the Spirit of the knowledge and the fear of You. May the Holy Spirit give him discernment in every decision he makes and turn his head in the right direction.

His Shoulders

But blessed is the man who trusts in the LORD, whose confidence is in him. He will be like a tree planted by the water that sends out its roots by the stream. It does not fear when heat comes; its leaves are always green. It has no worries in a year of drought and never fails to bear fruit. *Jeremiah 17:7–8*

Make my husband like a tree planted by streams of living water. When the economy goes bad, when his pay seems slim, when the bills pile high, I pray he will not feel burdened or anxious. Instead, show him how to sink his roots deep into the living water of Jesus, which never ebbs low or runs dry.

His Heart

A man of perverse heart does not prosper. *Proverbs 17:20*

Lord, please place a hedge of protection around my husband's heart to keep corruption from creeping in. Protect his heart from any inclination that would lead to dishonest gain, deceitful dealings, or truth-twisting entanglements. Help him root out any form of corruption that would prevent him from prospering and receiving Your bountiful blessings.

His Back

For we are not unaware of his [Satan's] schemes. *2 Corinthians 2:11*

Make my husband aware of the devil's schemes to trip him up and bring him down. Help him recognize the Enemy's strategically placed traps. Protect him from the devil's schemes, and intercept the Enemy's plans to bring him harm.

His Arms

O LORD, be gracious to us; we long for you. Be our strength every morning, our salvation in time of distress. *Isaiah 33:2*

Lord, I ask You to be gracious to my husband. Strengthen him every morning with Your power and might, and deliver him in times of distress with Your sure defense.

His Hands

From the fruit of his lips a man is filled with good things as surely as the work of his hands rewards him. *Proverbs 12:14*

I pray that my husband will see good things come from the work of his hands. Let him reap in full the fruit of his labor. May he be noticed, acknowledged, and praised for a job well done. Let him catch a glimpse of ways he has made a lasting impact at his workplace and in his sphere of influence.

His Ring Finger

Now I want you to realize that the head of every man is Christ, and the head of the woman is man, and the head of Christ is God. *1 Corinthians 11:3*

Lord, thank You for calling my husband to be the spiritual leader of our home. Show him how to lead with godly wisdom that comes straight from You. Help him be confident and courageous in his role as head of our home. Equip me to be a wife who does not balk at my husband's leadership but encourages it. Rather than my usurping his role, destroying his confidence, and always thinking I have a better idea, help me make it easy for him to be the leader You designed him to be.

His Side

[Jesus said,] "A new command I give you: Love one another. As I have loved you, so you must love one another." *John 13:34*

Empower my husband to love other people as Jesus has loved him—sacrificially, unconditionally, and with a servant's heart.

His Sexuality

Watch and pray so that you will not fall into temptation. The spirit is willing, but the body is weak. *Mark 14:38*

Please help my husband to be on the alert today, watching and praying so that he will not fall into temptation. Strengthen his spiritual and physical resolve to remain sexually pure.

His Legs

> For this is what the LORD says—he who created the heavens, he is God; he who fashioned and made the earth, he founded it; he did not create it to be empty, but formed it to be inhabited—he says: "I am the LORD, and there is no other." *Isaiah 45:18*

Lord, You are the One who created the heavens, who fashioned the earth and founded the seas. You speak the truth and declare what is right. I pray my husband will stand on Your truth and not be swayed, deceived, or confused by the world's ever-changing ideas of right and wrong. Don't let him teeter on the fence, but instead, plant him firmly on the rock of Your truth that is the same yesterday, today, and tomorrow. Help him remember that You are the Lord and there is no other solid place to stand.

His Knees

> He [God] testified concerning him: "I have found David son of Jesse a man after my own heart; he will do everything I want him to do." *Acts 13:22*

I pray my husband will not be a proud man who only pursues his own desires but a humble man who only wants what You want. Shape him into a man after Your own heart, one who kneels in total submission to Your will.

His Feet

> I have kept my feet from every evil path so that I might obey your word. *Psalm 119:101*

Direct my husband's feet away from every evil path so that he might obey Your Word. Keep him from straying to the left or the right, and help him stay on the roadway of right living paved with grace. In Jesus' name, amen.

Day Fifteen

His Mind

You were taught, with regard to your former way of life, to put
off your old self, which is being corrupted by its deceitful desires;
to be made new in the attitude of your minds; and to put on the new
self, created to be like God in true righteousness and holiness.
Ephesians 4:22–24

Heavenly Father, I pray my husband will continually put off the old self
and the old desires that meddle with his mind and tinker with his thought
life. Renew his mind with Your truth—align his thinking with Your
thinking and his attitude with Your attitude. Purify his mind so that it
becomes a reflection of Your righteousness and holiness.

His Eyes

Lift your eyes and look to the heavens: Who created all these? He who
brings out the starry host one by one, and calls them each by name.
Because of his great power and mighty strength, not one of them is
missing. *Isaiah 40:26*

Prompt my husband to lift up his eyes and look to the heavens. Help him
to see Your great power, mighty strength, and radiant glory in all of creation. Let him know that if You can take care of the tiniest dust particle
of heaven and hold the entire universe in balance, then You can take care
of him today.

His Ears

The Sovereign LORD...wakens me morning by morning, wakens my ear
to listen like one being taught. *Isaiah 50:4*

Sovereign Lord, waken my husband's ear to listen like one being taught. Increase his awareness of Your voice, and attune his senses to detect Your articulate presence all day long.

His Mouth

> But I tell you that men will have to give account on the day of judgment for every careless word they have spoken. For by your words you will be acquitted, and by your words you will be condemned. *Matthew 12:36–37*

Guard my husband's mouth so he will be acquitted by his words and not condemned. Remind him that he will be called to account on the Day of Judgment for every careless word he has spoken. Help him be mindful of the power of his words to affect his life and the lives of others.

His Neck

> Call to me and I will answer you and tell you great and unsearchable things you do not know. *Jeremiah 33:3*

When my husband has a difficult decision to make, I pray he will call to You and ask for guidance. Teach him great and unsearchable things he did not know. Give him insight and wisdom beyond human explanation and worldly understanding.

His Shoulders

> "For I know the plans I have for you," declares the LORD, "plans to prosper you and not to harm you, plans to give you hope and a future." *Jeremiah 29:11*

I thank You, Lord, that You have a good purpose and a perfect plan for my husband's life—a plan not to harm him but to give him hope and a future. Cause him to rest in the knowledge that You always have his best interests in mind.

His Heart

A cheerful heart is good medicine, but a crushed spirit dries up the bones. *Proverbs 17:22*

Please bless my husband with a cheerful, joyful, and positive heart—a heart that nourishes his body rather than drains his soul.

His Back

The angel of the LORD encamps around those who fear him, and he delivers them. *Psalm 34:7*

I pray the angel of the Lord will encamp around my husband today. Protect him in the physical and spiritual realms. Defend him against any snares of the Enemy that would trap him, tempt him, or trip him. Deliver him from any people purposed to harm him.

His Arms

He gives strength to the weary and increases the power of the weak. Even youths grow tired and weary, and young men stumble and fall; but those who hope in the LORD will renew their strength. They will soar on wings like eagles; they will run and not grow weary, they will walk and not be faint. *Isaiah 40:29–31*

Lord, when my husband grows weary today, give him the stamina to continue on. When he grows weak, give him strength to press forward. Enable him to soar on wings like eagles that drift along on the current You provide rather than flap ferociously to stay in flight. Give him energy to run and not grow weary, to walk and not be faint. May his hope in You bring power to his body, spirit, and soul.

His Hands

Do you see a man skilled in his work? He will serve before kings.

Proverbs 22:29

Equip my husband to be skilled in his work. Fill him with the power and wisdom of the Holy Spirit to do all things well. Give him favor, Lord, and may his good work be recognized and acknowledged by others.

His Ring Finger

Love is patient, love is kind. *1 Corinthians 13:4*

Lord, please bless our marriage with an abundance of patience and kindness. I pray my husband will be patient when I don't behave the way he would like, kind when I am difficult to live with, and gentle with me through the ups and downs of our life together. I pray I will be patient with my husband when he doesn't behave as I would like, kind when he is difficult to live with, and gentle with him through the ups and downs of our life together.

His Side

Love is patient, love is kind. It does not envy, it does not boast, it is not proud. It is not rude, it is not self-seeking, it is not easily angered, it keeps no record of wrongs. Love does not delight in evil but rejoices with the truth. It always protects, always trusts, always hopes, always perseveres. *1 Corinthians 13:4–7*

Just as I pray for my husband to be patient and kind with me, I pray that he will be patient and kind with his family, friends, and coworkers. Show him how to demonstrate a love that is not envious, boastful, proud, rude, self-seeking, or easily angered. Don't allow him to keep a record of wrongs, but empower him to quickly forgive and not bring it up again. May he not delight when things go wrong for others, but celebrate when things go right. Nurture in him a love for his family, friends, and coworkers that always protects, always trusts, always hopes, and always perseveres.

His Sexuality

> How handsome you are, my lover! Oh, how charming! And our bed is verdant. *Song of Songs 1:16*

Give me the words and ways to let my husband know that I am attracted to him and desire him sexually. Make our bed and times of intimacy as inviting and refreshing as a forest glen, a place he enjoys and longs to be.

His Legs

> On the contrary, we speak as men approved by God to be entrusted with the gospel. We are not trying to please men but God, who tests our hearts. *1 Thessalonians 2:4*

I pray my husband will not be afraid to stand up for the truth. Stir up a desire in him to please You above pleasing men.

His Knees

> Jesus replied, "If anyone loves me, he will obey my teaching. My Father will love him, and we will come to him and make our home with him." *John 14:23*

Jesus, stir my husband to show he loves You by obeying Your teaching. Help him to not be proud and go his own way but be humble and submit to Your better way.

His Feet

Your word is a lamp to my feet and a light for my path. *Psalm 119:105*

Let Your Word shine as a lamp for my husband's feet and a light on his path. May Your truth cast a bright beam that points him in the right direction today. I pray all this in Jesus' name, amen.

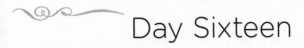

Day Sixteen

His Mind

> Then he [Jesus] opened their minds so they could understand the
> Scriptures. *Luke 24:45*

Heavenly Father, just as Jesus opened the minds of the disciples to understand the Scriptures, I ask that You open my husband's mind to understand Your Word. May the Holy Spirit be his teacher so that he will not
be confused by the Scriptures but enlightened. Pull up the shades, open
the shutters, turn on the lights! Connect the dots, and make the Scriptures clear to him.

His Eyes

> You will see it with your own eyes and say, "Great is the LORD—even
> beyond the borders of Israel!" *Malachi 1:5*

Open my husband's eyes to see You at work in his life today. Help him
recognize Your presence and power on display.

His Ears

> If my people would but listen to me, if Israel would follow my ways,
> how quickly would I subdue their enemies and turn my hand against
> their foes! *Psalm 81:13–14*

Increase my husband's spiritual ability to detect Your voice. I pray he will
not turn a deaf ear to Your commands but listen to the Holy Spirit's
promptings throughout the day. I ask that You quickly subdue the powers
of darkness that would seek to harm him. Turn Your hand against the
principalities of evil that intend to hurt him.

His Mouth

Jesus called the crowd to him and said, "Listen and understand. What goes into a man's mouth does not make him 'unclean,' but what comes out of his mouth, that is what makes him 'unclean.'" *Matthew 15:10–11*

Stir my husband's heart to be more concerned with what comes out of his mouth than what goes in. Make him keenly aware of the words he speaks and careful not to taint his reputation by the way he talks.

His Neck

This is what the LORD says—your Redeemer, the Holy One of Israel: "I am the LORD your God, who teaches you what is best for you, who directs you in the way you should go." *Isaiah 48:17*

Lord, I ask that You teach my husband what is best for him and help him make the best decisions possible. Lead him to turn his head away from potentially harmful decisions and toward assuredly helpful choices.

His Shoulders

Ask and it will be given to you; seek and you will find; knock and the door will be opened to you. For everyone who asks receives; he who seeks finds; and to him who knocks, the door will be opened. *Matthew 7:7–8*

When my husband has a need today, remind him that You would love for him to ask You for help rather than try to meet it on his own. Thank You for the promise that everyone who asks receives, he who seeks finds, and to him who knocks, the door will be opened.

His Heart

Let us draw near to God with a sincere heart in full assurance of faith, having our hearts sprinkled to cleanse us from a guilty conscience. *Hebrews 10:22*

Remind my husband that he can draw near to You with a sincere heart in full assurance of faith, knowing that his heart has been sanctified by the blood of the Lamb. I pray he will not cower in shame because of lingering guilt in his heart; rather, let him approach the throne with the confidence of a man whose slate has been wiped clean.

His Back

God is our refuge and strength, an ever-present help in trouble. Therefore we will not fear, though the earth give way and the mountains fall into the heart of the sea, though its waters roar and foam and the mountains quake with their surging. *Psalm 46:1–3*

God, thank You for being my husband's refuge and strength, an ever-present help in trouble. No matter what happens in his life today, even if his whole world seems to be falling apart around him, I pray You will keep him safe and secure.

His Arms

So do not fear, for I am with you; do not be dismayed, for I am your God. I will strengthen you and help you; I will uphold you with my righteous right hand. *Isaiah 41:10*

Encourage my husband to not fear or be dismayed, because You are with him. Remind him that You will strengthen him and help him. Uphold him, Father, with Your righteous right hand, no matter what difficult circumstance tries to pull him down.

His Hands

I know that there is nothing better for men than to be happy and do good while they live. That everyone may eat and drink, and find satisfaction in all his toil—this is the gift of God. *Ecclesiastes 3:12–13*

Lord, I pray my husband will be happy and do good while he lives. May he find satisfaction and fulfillment in his work. Help him view his work as something he *gets* to do and not as something he *has* to do. I pray he will see his job as a gift from You and will have a positive influence and lasting impact on all those he touches through his work.

His Ring Finger

Love...is not jealous. *1 Corinthians 13:4,* NASB

Protect my husband from becoming jealous of other people or interests in my life, but keep him secure in my love for him. Likewise, protect me from being jealous of other people or interests in my husband's life, but help me rest secure in his love for me.

His Side

Be devoted to one another in brotherly love. Honor one another above yourselves. *Romans 12:10*

Teach my husband to be devoted in brotherly love to his friends, family, and coworkers. Show him how to honor those with whom he walks side by side, giving them precedence and considering their desires above his own. I pray he will not mind playing second fiddle when a friend has the opportunity to play first chair.

His Sexuality

Hate what is evil; cling to what is good. *Romans 12:9*

Help my husband hate what is evil and cling to what is good. Prompt him to run away from what is sexually perverse and move toward what You have ordained and approved.

His Legs

> Shadrach, Meshach and Abednego replied to the king, "O Nebuchadnezzar, we do not need to defend ourselves before you in this matter. If we are thrown into the blazing furnace, the God we serve is able to save us from it, and he will rescue us from your hand, O king. But even if he does not, we want you to know, O king, that we will not serve your gods or worship the image of gold you have set up." *Daniel 3:16–18*

Like Shadrach, Meshach, and Abednego, who refused to bow to any god but You, I pray my husband will not be afraid to stand up against world systems and leaders that demand he deny his faith. Give him strength to stand firm in the truth of Your sovereign and supreme power. I pray You will stand with him in the fiery furnace of this world and bring him forth without a hint of smoke.

His Knees

> Pride goes before destruction, a haughty spirit before a fall.
> *Proverbs 16:18*

I pray my husband will not be prideful, haughty, or arrogant but that he will be humble, submissive, and malleable in Your hands. May his relationship with You be characterized by obedience that flows from a deep, abiding love.

His Feet

> Mark out a straight path for your feet; stay on the safe path. Don't get sidetracked; keep your feet from following evil. *Proverbs 4:26–27, NLT*

Guide my husband to mark out a straight path for his feet and stick to it. Help him ignore the world's sideshow distractions and stay on the safe, well-lit path of Christ. In Jesus' name, amen.

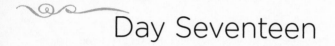

Day Seventeen

His Mind

I keep asking that the God of our Lord Jesus Christ, the glorious Father, may give you the Spirit of wisdom and revelation, so that you may know him better. *Ephesians 1:17*

I ask You to give my husband the Spirit of wisdom and revelation so that he may know You better. Enlighten his mind so that he will know You not just intellectually but also personally, intimately, and experientially.

His Eyes

But the LORD said to Samuel, "Do not consider his appearance or his height, for I have rejected him. The LORD does not look at the things man looks at. Man looks at the outward appearance, but the LORD looks at the heart." *1 Samuel 16:7*

Help my husband resist the inclination to judge people by their physical appearance. Teach him how to see men and women as You see them—as either a sanctified but imperfect brother or sister in Christ, or a lost person in need of Your saving grace.

His Ears

Listen to me, you who pursue righteousness and who seek the LORD: Look to the rock from which you were cut and to the quarry from which you were hewn. *Isaiah 51:1*

Heavenly Father, I pray my husband will listen to You, seek You, and pursue righteousness. Remind him that he is cut from the Rock of Jesus Christ and chosen from the quarry of Your living stones.

His Mouth

> For I will give you words and wisdom that none of
> your adversaries will be able to resist or contradict.
> *Luke 21:15*

Give my husband words and wisdom that none of his adversaries will be able to resist or contradict. May his words draw others in and not push them away. Show him how to speak about You in such a way that others will want to know more.

His Neck

> Plans fail for lack of counsel,
> but with many advisers they succeed.
> *Proverbs 15:22*

When my husband has a decision to make, direct him to godly men who can provide wise counsel.

His Shoulders

> Come to me, all you who are weary and burdened, and I will
> give you rest. Take my yoke upon you and learn from me,
> for I am gentle and humble in heart, and you will find rest
> for your souls. For my yoke is easy and my burden is light.
> *Matthew 11:28–30*

Jesus, when my husband feels overburdened with the cares of this world, I pray he will come to You and rest in You. I pray he will take off his yoke of self-sufficiency and put on the yoke of Christ-sufficiency. I pray he will throw off the self-imposed burden that he has to make life work on his own power and embrace the freeing truth that he can do all things through Christ who gives him strength.

His Heart

Do not let your heart envy sinners, but always be zealous for the fear of the LORD. There is surely a future hope for you, and your hope will not be cut off. *Proverbs 23:17–18*

Protect my husband's heart, and do not let him envy sinners who seem to be getting ahead or having fun. Teach him to be content and thankful for the ways You have provided for him. Help him not lose hope but to look forward to his future reward and eternal blessing that are sure to come.

His Back

He who dwells in the shelter of the Most High will rest in the shadow of the Almighty. I will say of the LORD, "He is my refuge and my fortress, my God, in whom I trust." *Psalm 91:1–2*

Most High God, I pray my husband will choose to dwell in the shelter of Your protection and rest in the shadow of Your care. Teach him to say with confidence, "The Lord is my refuge and my fortress, my God in whom I trust."

His Arms

The LORD will guide you always; he will satisfy your needs in a sun-scorched land and will strengthen your frame. You will be like a well-watered garden, like a spring whose waters never fail. *Isaiah 58:11*

Father, strengthen my husband's body and protect his health. I pray he will not wither like grass in sun-parched ground but thrive like a strong fruit tree in a well-watered garden.

His Hands

> Strengthen the feeble hands, steady the knees that give way.
> *Isaiah 35:3*

When my husband feels inferior, insecure, or inadequate at work, I ask You to strengthen his feeble hands and steady his weak knees. Give him confidence, security, and courage to work with the steadfast hands of a man who is sure of his God-given abilities and talents.

His Ring Finger

> [Love] keeps no record of wrongs. *1 Corinthians 13:5*

Don't allow my husband or me to keep a running record of each other's mistakes and failures, but help us forgive each offense and then not bring it up again. Stop us from keeping a mental list of offenses, and help us to toss each one into the deepest of seas, the same place where You toss our forgiven sins.

His Side

> Make up your mind not to put any stumbling block or obstacle in your brother's way. *Romans 14:13*

Help my husband give priority to the spiritual health of fellow believers rather than cling to his personal rights. Give him the determination to not speak any words or exhibit any behavior that would create a stumbling block or obstacle for another person's spiritual journey.

His Sexuality

> Because we belong to the day, we must live decent lives for all to see. Don't participate in the darkness of wild parties and drunkenness, or in sexual promiscuity and immoral

> living, or in quarreling and jealousy. Instead, clothe
> yourself with the presence of the Lord Jesus Christ.
> And don't let yourself think about ways to indulge
> your evil desires. *Romans 13:13–14,* NLT

I pray my husband will behave decently and honorably for all to see. Keep him from thinking about or participating in any immoral sexual behavior. Take away any evil cravings, and replace them with godly desires. Show him how to clothe himself in the presence of the Lord Jesus Christ and live a life reflective of You.

His Legs

> Jesus replied, "I tell you the truth, if you have faith
> and do not doubt, not only can you do what was done
> to the fig tree, but also you can say to this mountain,
> 'Go, throw yourself into the sea,' and it will be done.
> If you believe, you will receive whatever you ask for in
> prayer." *Matthew 21:21–22*

Strengthen my husband's faith so that he will stand on Your promises doubt-free. Give him the type of faith that moves mountains. I pray he will believe and receive whatever he asks for in prayer that is according to Your perfect will.

His Knees

> "As surely as I live," says the Lord, "every knee will bow before me;
> every tongue will confess to God." *Romans 14:11*

Humble my husband to bend his knee in submission to You and in worship of You. Remove any pride or arrogance that would hinder him from experiencing a maturing relationship with You.

His Feet

The man of integrity walks securely, but he who takes crooked paths will be found out. *Proverbs 10:9*

Equip my husband to be a man of integrity who walks securely on the road of moral character paved with Your truth, and keep him from the lure of crooked paths. In Jesus' name, amen.

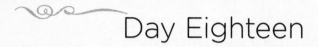

Day Eighteen

His Mind

> I pray that you, being rooted and established in love, may have power, together with all the saints, to grasp how wide and long and high and deep is the love of Christ, and to know this love that surpasses knowledge—that you may be filled to the measure of all the fullness of God. *Ephesians 3:17–19*

Almighty God, I pray that my husband, being rooted and established in love, may have the power, together with all the saints, to grasp how wide and long and high and deep is the love of Christ, and to know this love that surpasses knowledge—that he may be filled to the measure of all the fullness of You. Enable his mind to grasp the concept of Your love for him even though the full measure of it is far beyond human understanding.

His Eyes

> The eye is the lamp of the body. If your eyes are good, your whole body will be full of light. But if your eyes are bad, your whole body will be full of darkness. If then the light within you is darkness, how great is that darkness! *Matthew 6:22–23*

Lord, Your Word tells us that what we look at affects our entire being. Guide my husband to open his eyes to things that shine Your light into his soul, and close them to that which would snuff it out.

His Ears

> Consequently, faith comes from hearing the message, and the message is heard through the word of Christ.
> *Romans 10:17*

Among all the things clamoring for my husband's attention today, help him tune his ear to that which will further his faith and bolster his belief. Mature his faith as a direct result of what and who he listens to.

His Mouth

> Instead, speaking the truth in love, we will in all things grow up into him who is the Head, that is, Christ. *Ephesians 4:15*

Teach my husband how to speak the truth in love. If he has to confront a coworker, a friend, or even me, prompt him to sift his words through the filter of mercy and grace before he speaks.

His Neck

> He gives wisdom to the wise and knowledge to the discerning. *Daniel 2:21*

Lord, just as You gave Daniel wisdom to make the best decisions, even when it meant contradicting the culture in which he lived, I ask You to give my husband Your wisdom to make the best decisions despite the culture in which he lives. Bless him with supernatural knowledge and spot-on discernment for every choice he makes today.

His Shoulders

> The one who received the seed that fell among the thorns is the man who hears the word, but the worries of this life and the deceitfulness of wealth choke it, making it unfruitful. But the one who received the seed that fell on good soil is the man who hears the word and understands it. He produces a crop, yielding a hundred, sixty or thirty times what was sown. *Matthew 13:22–23*

Help my husband to not let the worries of this life or the deceitfulness of wealth choke out Your Word planted in his heart. Teach him how to weed out worry and cultivate understanding in order to produce a bumper crop of good fruit.

His Heart

Blessed is the man who always fears the LORD, but he who hardens his heart falls into trouble. *Proverbs 28:14*

Lord, give my husband a malleable heart. May he always fear You, revere You, and submit to You. Keep his heart from becoming hardened through any form of disobedience or rebellion against You.

His Back

He will cover you with his feathers. He will shelter you with his wings. His faithful promises are your armor and protection. *Psalm 91:4,* NLT

Thank You, God, for Your protective presence. Cover my husband with Your feathers and shelter him with Your mighty wings as a mother hen protects her chicks. Let Your faithful promises be my husband's armor and sure defense.

His Arms

Do not grieve, for the joy of the LORD is your strength.
Nehemiah 8:10

I pray my husband will not be grieved or dismayed because of his weaknesses but rejoice and be glad because of Your strength. Help him focus not on his own insufficiencies but on Your all-sufficiency.

His Hands

When he had finished speaking, he said to Simon, "Put out into deep water, and let down the nets for a catch." Simon answered, "Master, we've worked hard all night and haven't caught anything.

But because you say so, I will let down the nets." When they had
done so, they caught such a large number of fish that their nets
began to break. *Luke 5:4–6*

Lord, we can be like Simon, who worked hard all night and still came
up empty handed. Or we can cast our nets where You tell us to cast
them and bring in record-breaking results. Help my husband know
exactly where to cast his nets. I pray he will ask You for clear direction
at work and then follow those directions to a T—even if they don't
make sense to him. Give him the faith to say with Simon, "Because you
say so, I will."

His Ring Finger

[Love] always protects, always trusts, always hopes, always perseveres. Love never fails. *1 Corinthians 13:7–8*

Lord, give my husband a love for me that always protects, always trusts,
and always perseveres. Likewise, I pray my love for him bears up under
anything and everything that comes our way. No matter what happens,
help us believe the best and hope the best for each other. May our love
never fail—never fade with time or wane with age.

His Side

Accept one another, then, just as Christ accepted you, in order to
bring praise to God. *Romans 15:7*

Help my husband accept others, just as Christ accepted him—totally
and unconditionally.

His Sexuality

Like a city whose walls are broken down is a man who lacks self-control.
Proverbs 25:28

Empower my husband to exercise self-control in the area of his sexuality. I pray he will not be like an ancient city with broken-down walls or an unprotected house with all the doors and windows knocked out, but that he will be like a fortified city and a well-protected home, locked and bolted against the enemy.

His Legs

But Peter and John replied, "Judge for yourselves whether it is right in God's sight to obey you rather than God. For we cannot help speaking about what we have seen and heard." *Acts 4:19–20*

Give my husband the courage to stand for truth in the face of persecution, rejection, or disapproval. Help him to always obey You rather than men.

His Knees

For this reason also, God highly exalted Him, and bestowed on Him the name which is above every name, so that at the name of Jesus every knee will bow, of those who are in heaven and on earth and under the earth, and that every tongue will confess that Jesus Christ is Lord, to the glory of God the Father. *Philippians 2:9–11,* NASB

I pray my husband will bow his knee and confess that Jesus Christ is Lord of every area of his life. Empower him to hold nothing back.

His Feet

He who walks with the wise grows wise, but a companion of fools suffers harm. *Proverbs 13:20*

Bring wise people into my husband's life—people from whom he can learn as they walk side by side. Protect him from falling in step with fools, and connect him with those who will encourage him to walk in tandem with You. In Jesus' name, amen.

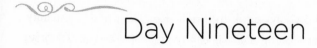

Day Nineteen

His Mind

I pray also that the eyes of your heart may be enlightened in order that you may know the hope to which he has called you, the riches of his glorious inheritance in the saints, and his incomparably great power for us who believe. *Ephesians 1:18–19*

I pray the eyes of my husband's heart will be enlightened in order that he may know the hope to which You have called him, the riches of Your glorious inheritance in the saints, and Your incomparably great power for us who believe. Help him grasp what it means to be a child of God: chosen, forgiven, redeemed, sanctified, and eventually glorified. May he comprehend the immensity of the glorious way of life You have for Your followers and the lavish extravagance of Your work in the lives of those who trust You.

His Eyes

Blessed are your eyes because they see. *Matthew 13:16*

Open my husband's eyes to see You today. May he experience moments of sudden glory in which he recognizes Your presence and Your work in his life.

His Ears

Blessed are…your ears because they hear. *Matthew 13:16*

Attune my husband's ears to hear from You today. Help him to recognize Your voice speaking to his heart and to listen carefully to all You say.

His Mouth

Therefore each of you must put off falsehood and speak truthfully to his neighbor, for we are all members of one body. *Ephesians 4:25*

Help my husband always speak truthfully. Keep him from stretching, distorting, or embellishing the facts of any situation. May his words be honest and honorable.

His Neck

> So David inquired of the LORD, and he answered. *2 Samuel 5:23*

When my husband has a tough decision to make today, prompt him to pray. Thank You for answering him when he calls to You.

His Shoulders

> Jesus looked at them and said, "With man this is impossible,
> but with God all things are possible." *Matthew 19:26*

Dear Lord, increase my husband's faith so that he will rest in the assurance that everything is possible for him who believes. Remove any unbelief and uncertainty in his heart, and help him see that there is no burden too heavy for Your shoulders to bear, no sickness too grave for You to heal, no problem too complicated for You to solve, no heart too broken for You to mend.

His Heart

> I will give them an undivided heart and put a new spirit in them;
> I will remove from them their heart of stone and give them a
> heart of flesh. *Ezekiel 11:19*

Loving Lord, please give my husband an undivided heart. Keep him from having a fickle heart that is half in Your camp and half in the world's. Give him an excitement and determination to be sold out to Jesus 100 percent. Soften any areas of his heart that have become hardened through the years, and sensitize his heart to the promptings of the Holy Spirit.

His Back

Though a thousand fall at your side, though ten thousand are dying around you, these evils will not touch you. *Psalm 91:7,* NLT

Even though it may seem the world is falling apart around him, help my husband rest secure in Your protection and provision. Shield him from danger and rescue him from harm.

His Arms

Let the weak say, "I am strong." *Joel 3:10,* NKJV

When my husband feels weak, weary, and worn out, remind him to draw on Your strength and mighty power.

His Hands

Let us not become weary in doing good, for at the proper time we will reap a harvest if we do not give up. *Galatians 6:9*

If my husband ever feels weary in doing good, give him the stamina to press on, knowing that he will reap a harvest at the proper time if he does not give up.

His Ring Finger

Be completely humble and gentle; be patient, bearing with one another in love. *Ephesians 4:2*

Show my husband and me how to be completely humble, gentle, and patient with each other, bearing with each other in love.

His Side

Do not be misled: "Bad company corrupts good character."
1 Corinthians 15:33

Protect my husband from forming close relationships or alliances with ungodly or unprincipled men. Help him remember that bad company corrupts good character and that spending time with immoral men will affect his attitude, words, and behavior. Give him close friends who will influence him to be a man of high moral character and deep, abiding faith.

His Sexuality

> Do you not know that your body is a temple of the Holy Spirit, who
> is in you, whom you have received from God? You are not your own;
> you were bought at a price. Therefore honor God with your body.
>
> *1 Corinthians 6:19–20*

Remind my husband that his body is a temple of the Holy Spirit, who resides in him and works through him. Empower him to keep his temple sexually pure. Help him remember that his body is not his own but that he was bought at a high price.

His Legs

> Without weakening in his faith, he [Abraham] faced the fact
> that his body was as good as dead—since he was about a hundred
> years old—and that Sarah's womb was also dead. Yet he did not
> waver through unbelief regarding the promise of God, but was
> strengthened in his faith and gave glory to God, being fully
> persuaded that God had power to do what he had promised.
>
> *Romans 4:19–21*

Teach my husband how to be a modern-day Abraham—a man who does not waver in unbelief regarding Your promises but stands firm in his faith, being fully persuaded that You have the power to do what You have promised.

His Knees

> But after Uzziah became powerful, his pride led to his downfall.
>
> *2 Chronicles 26:16*

Keep my husband from ever becoming prideful because of his accomplishments, but guide him to remain humble and grateful for Your provision and blessing.

His Feet

> In his heart a man plans his course, but the LORD determines his steps.
>
> *Proverbs 16:9*

Lord, as my husband makes his plans and plots his course through life, I pray You will direct his decisions and determine his steps. In Jesus' name, amen.

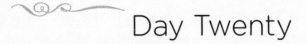

Day Twenty

His Mind

[Isaiah asked,] "For who has known the mind of the Lord
that he may instruct him?" But we have the mind of Christ.
1 Corinthians 2:16

Heavenly Father, Your ways are higher than our ways and Your thoughts are higher than our thoughts. They are beyond human understanding. However, the Bible tells us that believers have the mind of Christ. I pray my husband will align his thoughts with Christ's thoughts, his reasoning with Christ's reasoning, and his purposes with Christ's purposes.

His Eyes

Watch and pray so that you will not fall into temptation.
The spirit is willing, but the flesh is weak. *Matthew 26:41,*
NIV 2011

Keep my husband alert and on guard so that he won't fall into temptation. Don't let him grow overconfident or be underprepared, but make him mindful of flesh's weaknesses and the Enemy's schemes to tempt him through what he sees. Strengthen his self-control so that his physical ability to divert his eyes from temptation matches his spiritual desire to honor You.

His Ears

But they did not listen or pay attention; instead, they followed the
stubborn inclinations of their evil hearts. They went backward and not
forward. *Jeremiah 7:24*

Lord, sharpen my husband's ability to hear from You. Keep him from listening to the stubborn inclinations of the flesh, and help him to heed the Holy Spirit within him. Turn his ear to listen to and obey Your commands so that he will not go backward but move forward.

His Mouth

Do not let any unwholesome talk come out of your mouths, but only what is helpful for building others up according to their needs, that it may benefit those who listen. *Ephesians 4:29*

Lord, give my husband the discipline to keep any unwholesome talk from coming out of his mouth and only speak words that are helpful for building others up according to their needs. Keep any foul language, unclean jokes, or coarse jesting from escaping the door of his lips, and let only speech that is good, clean, and beneficial to others be spoken.

His Neck

And I will walk at liberty and at ease, for I have sought and inquired for [and desperately required] Your precepts. *Psalm 119:45,* AMP

In all my husband's decisions today, prompt him to seek Your will and frame his choices in the context of Your truth.

His Shoulders

The next day Moses took his seat to serve as judge for the people, and they stood around him from morning till evening. When his father-in-law saw all that Moses was doing for the people, he said,…"What you are doing is not good. You and these people who come to you will only wear yourselves out. The work is too heavy for you; you cannot handle it alone." *Exodus 18:13–14, 17–18*

Lord, I pray my husband will not feel as though he has to tackle every task that comes his way but that he will do what only he can do and seek out capable, trustworthy people to share the load. Show him when to delegate responsibility so that he can do his best at the work You have called him to do.

His Heart

For where your treasure is, there your heart will be also. *Matthew 6:21*

I know that what my husband treasures in his heart is where he will spend his time, resources, and energy. Therefore, I pray he will fill the safety deposit box of his heart with treasures that cannot be stolen, will not rust, and will not lose value in a fluctuating economy. Remind him that the most valuable treasure of all, the pearl of great price, is found in a loving relationship with You.

His Back

For he will command his angels concerning you to guard you in all your ways; they will lift you up in their hands, so that you will not strike your foot against a stone. *Psalm 91:11–12*

Loving Lord, thank You for Your angels who guard and protect my husband wherever he goes. I pray they will lift him up in their hands so he won't strike his foot against a stone, catch him if he stumbles, and brace him up so he won't fall. Protect him in the physical and spiritual realms so that no evil will harm him or prevail against him.

His Arms

If anyone serves, he should do it with the strength God provides, so that in all things God may be praised through Jesus Christ.
1 Peter 4:11

I pray my husband will not do anything in his own strength but with the strength You provide, so that in all things Your presence will be evident and You will be praised.

His Hands

> For we are God's workmanship, created in Christ Jesus to
> do good works, which God prepared in advance for us to do.
> *Ephesians 2:10*

Thank You for Your wonderful workmanship which I see in my husband. Reveal to him the work You have created him to do, and teach him how to do it with excellence.

His Ring Finger

> Make every effort to keep the unity of the Spirit through the bond of
> peace. *Ephesians 4:3*

Lord, help my husband and me make every effort to keep the unity of the Spirit in our marriage. Prompt us to express ourselves in ways that would not pull us apart and cause disharmony but to choose words and actions that would draw us closer together and foster peace.

His Side

> Do not be yoked together with unbelievers. For what do righteousness
> and wickedness have in common? Or what fellowship can light have
> with darkness? *2 Corinthians 6:14*

I pray my husband will not form a partnership with someone who rejects You. May he, as a child of the Light, not be legally yoked to a child of darkness, no matter how beneficial the partnership may seem on paper.

His Sexuality

> The husband should fulfill his marital duty to his wife, and likewise the wife to her husband.... Do not deprive each other except by mutual consent and for a time, so that you may devote yourselves to prayer. Then come together again so that Satan will not tempt you because of your lack of self-control. *1 Corinthians 7:3, 5*

Keep our marriage bed a place of mutual satisfaction where we both seek to please the other. May our sexual intimacy be precious and healthy so that unmet needs will not give Satan an opportunity to tempt us.

His Legs

> Now, brothers, I want to remind you of the gospel I preached to you, which you received and on which you have taken your stand. *1 Corinthians 15:1*

Strengthen my husband to stand firm on the gospel of Jesus Christ, and protect him from being shaken by the world, the flesh, or the devil.

His Knees

> When you have eaten and are satisfied, praise the LORD your God for the good land he has given you.... You may say to yourself, "My power and the strength of my hands have produced this wealth for me." But remember the LORD your God, for it is he who gives you the ability to produce wealth. *Deuteronomy 8:10, 17–18*

Lord, while I pray my husband will be successful and influential, I also pray that he will remain humble and grateful. Keep him from becoming prideful in his accomplishments, and help him remember that You give him the ability, provide him the opportunity, and bless his ingenuity.

His Feet

> The LORD says, "I will guide you along the best pathway for your life. I will advise you and watch over you." *Psalm 32:8,* NLT

Gracious Lord, please guide my husband along the best pathway for his life. Advise him and watch over his every step along the way. In Jesus' name, amen.

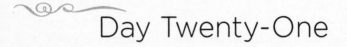

Day Twenty-One

His Mind

> But one thing I do: Forgetting what is behind and straining toward
> what is ahead, I press on toward the goal to win the prize for which
> God has called me heavenward in Christ Jesus. *Philippians 3:13–14*

Sovereign Lord, keep my husband from dwelling on the past. Purge his mind of thoughts of past sins that bring shame, prior offenses that bring bitterness, or missed opportunities that bring regret. Help him focus on what's ahead: the exciting journey of becoming all You have created him to be and doing all You have planned for him to do.

His Eyes

> "What do you want me to do for you?" Jesus asked him. The blind man
> said, "Rabbi, I want to see." *Mark 10:51*

Though my husband may not be physically blind, please give him a longing to see You and Your ways more clearly. May he say with the blind beggar, "Lord, I want to see."

His Ears

> You warned them to return to your law, but they became arrogant and
> disobeyed your commands. They sinned against your ordinances, by
> which a man will live if he obeys them. Stubbornly they turned their
> backs on you, became stiff-necked and refused to listen. *Nehemiah 9:29*

Keep my husband from being arrogant or proud. Stir in him a desire and determination to listen to and obey Your commands. Protect him from experiencing the devastating consequences of those who refuse to listen, and shower him with the blessings of those who do.

His Mouth

> Get rid of all bitterness, rage and anger, brawling and slander, along with every form of malice. Be kind and compassionate to one another, forgiving each other, just as in Christ God forgave you. *Ephesians 4:31–32*

Please keep my husband's conversation free of all bitterness, rage, anger, harsh words, and slander, along with every form of malice. If someone hurts, offends, or angers him, give him the power to hold his tongue and not retaliate with harsh words but respond with grace-filled speech.

His Neck

> For the foolishness of God is wiser than man's wisdom, and the weakness of God is stronger than man's strength. *1 Corinthians 1:25*

Lord, it is so easy to make decisions based on worldly wisdom and what seems to make sense at the moment, but I pray my husband will make decisions based on Your guidance, knowing You are always wiser than man's best efforts.

His Shoulders

> For nothing is impossible with God. *Luke 1:37*

I am so thankful that nothing, absolutely nothing, is impossible for You. When my husband straps the burden of self-sufficiency on his shoulders, prompt him to cut it loose and place it on Your shoulders where it belongs. Remove his worries and fears, and replace them with peace and trust. Assure him that nothing is too heavy for You to carry, too difficult for You to fix, too broken for You to mend.

His Heart

> Jesus replied: "'Love the Lord your God with all your heart and with all your soul and with all your mind.'" *Matthew 22:37*

I pray my husband will love You with all his heart and with all his soul and with all his mind—with his entire being. Show him anyone or anything that he loves more than You, and give him the wisdom and will to move them to their proper position in his heart and place his love for You above all else.

His Back

The LORD says, "I will rescue those who love me. I will protect those who trust in my name." *Psalm 91:14,* NLT

Holy Father, stir my husband to love You and trust You more today than he did yesterday. Rescue him when he is in danger, and protect him from harm.

His Arms

But you will receive power when the Holy Spirit comes on you. *Acts 1:8*

Father, thank You for the promised Holy Spirit who indwells all believers. I ask that my husband will be empowered by, filled with, and motivated by the power of the Holy Spirit in his life today. Deliver him from the tendency to depend on his own strength, and prompt him to access the power of the Holy Spirit who works in him and through him.

His Hands

Do everything without complaining or arguing, so that you may become blameless and pure, children of God without fault in a crooked and depraved generation, in which you shine like stars in the universe. *Philippians 2:14–15*

Help my husband tackle the tasks of his day without grumbling, arguing, or complaining. May his positive attitude shine as a bright light in a dark world.

His Ring Finger

> "In your anger do not sin": Do not let the sun go down while
> you are still angry, and do not give the devil a foothold.
>
> *Ephesians 4:26–27*

Lord, keep my husband and me from ever going to bed angry. Even though we may not be able to resolve every conflict before the sun goes down, help us to ask for forgiveness quickly and grant forgiveness completely. I pray we will not allow unresolved anger to provide a toehold for Satan in our marriage.

His Side

> "In your anger do not sin": Do not let the sun go down while
> you are still angry, and do not give the devil a foothold.
>
> *Ephesians 4:26–27*

Just as I prayed for the sun not to go down while my husband and I are still angry, I ask the same for his other relationships. When he gets upset or angry with a family member, friend, or coworker, soften his heart to seek prompt resolution. Help him to not go to bed angry, even if the issue is not resolved completely. Keep him from holding a grudge, plotting revenge, replaying the offense, or refusing to let it go. Don't allow him to give the devil a foothold in his life through anger, bitterness, or unforgiveness.

His Sexuality

> No temptation has seized you except what is common to man.
> And God is faithful; he will not let you be tempted beyond
> what you can bear. But when you are tempted, he will also
> provide a way out so that you can stand up under it.
>
> *1 Corinthians 10:13*

God, thank You for not allowing my husband to be tempted beyond what he can bear. Open his eyes to quickly recognize Your way of escape and make a clean getaway.

His Legs

> But thanks be to God! He gives us the victory through our Lord Jesus Christ. Therefore, my dear brothers, stand firm. Let nothing move you.
> *1 Corinthians 15:57–58*

God, thank You for giving us the victory over death through Jesus Christ's resurrection. Help my husband to stand firm in this truth, and let no one and nothing undermine his courage or shake his faith.

His Knees

> Be filled with the Spirit. *Ephesians 5:18*

Give my husband a fresh anointing and infilling of the Holy Spirit today. Infuse him with the Holy Spirit's peace and power anew.

His Feet

> Whether you turn to the right or to the left, your ears will hear a voice behind you, saying, "This is the way; walk in it." *Isaiah 30:21*

Lord, wherever my husband goes today, make his inner man sensitive to Your voice saying, "This is the way; walk in it." Guide him to faithfully follow Your nudging and not be distracted by the world's bells and whistles. May Your Word be his road map and Your Holy Spirit his guide. In Jesus' name, amen.

Day Twenty-Two

His Mind

My purpose is that they may be encouraged in heart and united in love, so that they may have the full riches of complete understanding, in order that they may know the mystery of God, namely, Christ, in whom are hidden all the treasures of wisdom and knowledge.

Colossians 2:2–3

Lord, I pray that my husband will grasp the full benefit of complete understanding of the gospel so that he can know intellectually and experientially all that You have done for him through Jesus' death and resurrection. Show him the hidden treasures of wisdom and knowledge that are waiting to be discovered in Christ.

His Eyes

Jesus entered Jericho and was passing through. A man was there by the name of Zacchaeus; he was a chief tax collector and was wealthy. He wanted to see who Jesus was, but being a short man he could not, because of the crowd. So he ran ahead and climbed a sycamore-fig tree to see him, since Jesus was coming that way. *Luke 19:1–4*

Just as Zacchaeus climbed the sycamore tree to get a better view of Jesus, I pray that my husband will do whatever it takes to see Jesus in his own life. Help him to remove what needs to be removed and add in what needs to be added so that he can see You clearly.

His Ears

Jesus said to him, "Away from me, Satan! For it is written..."

Matthew 4:10

Lord, keep my husband from listening to Satan's offers of quick power, easy success, or plentiful possessions. Help him shut out the lies of the Enemy by overcoming them with the Truth.

His Mouth

Nor should there be obscenity, foolish talk or coarse joking, which are out of place, but rather thanksgiving. *Ephesians 5:4*

Empower my husband to refrain from obscene speech, foolish talk, coarse joking, cursing, and swearing, and make his words honorable and upright. Fill his mouth with words of thanksgiving and praise.

His Neck

Do not deceive yourselves. If any one of you thinks he is wise by the standards of this age, he should become a "fool" so that he may become wise. For the wisdom of this world is foolishness in God's sight. *1 Corinthians 3:18–19*

Father, protect my husband from being deceived into thinking he is wise according to the world's standards, but make him truly wise according to Your standards.

His Shoulders

Consider how the lilies grow. They do not labor or spin. Yet I tell you, not even Solomon in all his splendor was dressed like one of these. If that is how God clothes the grass of the field, which is here today, and tomorrow is thrown into the fire, how much more will he clothe you, O you of little faith! *Luke 12:27–28*

Loving Lord, assure my husband that he does not need to worry about the details of life, such as what our family will eat or what we will wear.

Help him to do his best and leave the outcome to You. Remind him of how You take care of the lilies of the field, and help him trust that You will take care of him as well.

His Heart

> [Jesus said,] "Do not let your hearts be troubled.
> Trust in God; trust also in me." *John 14:1*

Keep my husband's heart from being worried or anxious about the future. Increase his faith so that he will trust in Your unfailing love, Your inexhaustible resources, and Your impermeable protection.

His Back

> The LORD will keep you from all harm—
> he will watch over your life;
> the LORD will watch over your coming and going
> both now and forevermore. *Psalm 121:7–8*

Lord, thank You for keeping my husband from all harm and watching over his entire life. Thank You for watching over his coming and going—both now and forevermore. Help my husband rest in the assurance of Your watchful eye and protective care.

His Arms

> For the kingdom of God is not a matter of talk but of power.
> *1 Corinthians 4:20*

I pray my husband will not just talk about Your power but believe it, access it, and exercise it. Let him experience the unmistakable working of Your mighty strength in his life. Embolden him to be strong and courageous to do all You have called him to do.

His Hands

I can do everything through him [Jesus] who gives me strength.
Philippians 4:13

Help my husband face every task with the confidence that Jesus is working in him and through him. Help him to remember and believe the promise that he can do all things You have called him to do through Christ who gives him strength.

His Ring Finger

Bear with each other and forgive whatever grievances you may have against one another. Forgive as the Lord forgave you. *Colossians 3:13*

Lord, fill my husband and me with mercy and grace so that we will be kind, compassionate, and quick to forgive each other, just as You have forgiven us. Enable us to forgive each other completely, not fishing out offenses from the deepest of seas into which You have tossed them or rewriting offenses on the pages where You have erased them.

His Side

Carry each other's burdens, and in this way you will fulfill the law of Christ. *Galatians 6:2*

When a friend, family member, or coworker has a burden that is too heavy to bear alone, prompt my husband to lend a helping hand, offer a strong back, or reach out with a caring heart. Teach him how to be Jesus' hands and feet to those in need.

His Sexuality

Therefore, if anyone is in Christ, he is a new creation; the old has gone, the new has come! *2 Corinthians 5:17*

Lord, thank You that my husband is a new creation in Christ. I pray he will not feel shame or condemnation from past sexual sins but cling to the truth that he is forgiven and free—the old has gone and the new has come.

His Legs

Be on your guard; stand firm in the faith; be men of courage; be strong. *1 Corinthians 16:13*

Almighty God, help my husband to stay alert and be on guard against anything or anyone that would seek to do him harm. Give him the strength and stamina to stand firm in his faith through the ups and downs of life. Increase his faith and make him a man of courage and confidence who does not buckle under pressure or temptation but holds his ground.

His Knees

Your attitude should be the same as that of Christ Jesus: Who, being in very nature God, did not consider equality with God something to be grasped, but made himself nothing, taking the very nature of a servant, being made in human likeness. And being found in appearance as a man, he humbled himself and became obedient to death—even death on a cross! *Philippians 2:5–8*

Just as Jesus set aside His privileges of deity and took on the status of a servant, I pray my husband will set aside his perceived rights, position, and pride to humbly serve others and obey You.

His Feet

For this God is our God for ever and ever; he will be our guide even to the end. *Psalm 48:14*

Eternal God, guide my husband's every step. Be his Shepherd who prods him forward when he lags behind and pulls him back when he runs ahead. Thank You for leading him all the days of his life. In Jesus' name, amen.

Day Twenty-Three

His Mind

> See to it that no one takes you captive through hollow and
> deceptive philosophy, which depends on human tradition
> and the basic principles of this world rather than on Christ.
> *Colossians 2:8*

Heavenly Father, protect my husband's mind from being taken captive by intellectual arguments, human reasoning, or deceptive philosophy. Guard his mind from anything that attempts to erase or negate the infallibility of God's truth.

His Eyes

> On reaching the place, he [Jesus] said to them, "Pray that you will not
> fall into temptation." *Luke 22:40*

I pray that my husband will not fall into temptation. Help him pay attention to the promptings of the Holy Spirit to turn his eyes away from anything or any person that would tempt him to sin. Keep him alert to and on guard against the schemes of the devil, knowing that the Enemy would love to snag him when he least expects it.

His Ears

> But blessed are your eyes because they see, and your ears because
> they hear. *Matthew 13:16*

Tune my husband's ears to the timbre of Your gentle whisper. Give him a discerning spirit to know the difference between Your voice and the world's voice speaking to his inner man.

His Mouth

> He who guards his mouth and his tongue keeps himself from calamity.
> *Proverbs 21:23*

Give my husband the wisdom and the will to guard his mouth today. Show him how to stay out of trouble by knowing when to speak and when to keep silent.

His Neck

> Paul and his companions traveled throughout the region of Phrygia and Galatia, having been kept by the Holy Spirit from preaching the word in the province of Asia. When they came to the border of Mysia, they tried to enter Bithynia, but the Spirit of Jesus would not allow them to. *Acts 16:6–7*

As my husband makes decisions about where he is to go and what he is to do, increase his sensitivity to the Holy Spirit holding him back or waving him forward.

His Shoulders

> And do not set your heart on what you will eat or drink; do not worry about it. For the pagan world runs after all such things, and your Father knows that you need them. But seek his kingdom, and these things will be given to you as well. *Luke 12:29–31*

How easily we let the hunger of our soul rumble with our culture's cravings. Rather than craving what will never satisfy his deepest longings, help my husband trust that You know exactly what he needs. May his relationship with You be his number-one priority. Lead him to seek You and Your kingdom first and foremost, knowing everything else will fall into place.

His Heart

> Do not love the world or anything in the world. If anyone loves
> the world, the love of the Father is not in him. For everything
> in the world—the cravings of sinful man, the lust of his eyes
> and the boasting of what he has and does—comes not from
> the Father but from the world. The world and its desires pass
> away, but the man who does the will of God lives forever.
> *1 John 2:15–17*

Deepen my husband's love for You today. Keep him from loving the world or anything in it more than he loves You. Help him to recognize and remember that the cravings of sinful man—the lust of his eyes and the boasting of what he has and does—do not come from You but from the world. May he be a man who does Your will and looks forward to eternal treasure.

His Back

> As the mountains surround Jerusalem,
> so the LORD surrounds his people
> both now and forevermore. *Psalm 125:2*

Lord, I ask You to surround my husband like a protective mountain range, both now and forevermore. Envelop him in Your protective presence.

His Arms

> But we have this treasure in jars of clay to show that this all-surpassing
> power is from God and not from us. *2 Corinthians 4:7*

Strengthen my husband—a simple jar of clay—to be a vessel filled with the all-surpassing power of the Holy Spirit.

His Hands

> And whatever you do, whether in word or deed, do it all in the name of the Lord Jesus, giving thanks to God the Father through him. *Colossians 3:17*

Whatever my husband does at work today, whether in the words he speaks or the tasks he performs, I pray he will do it all in the name of the Lord Jesus, giving thanks to You every step of the way.

His Ring Finger

> For the husband is the head of the wife as Christ is the head of the church, his body, of which he is the Savior. *Ephesians 5:23*

Lord, thank You that You have purposed my husband to be the head of our home, as Christ is the head of the Church. Bless him with wisdom, courage, and passion to lead our family. Show me any ways that I am hindering or usurping his leadership, and help me stop it right away. Instruct me in how I can encourage him in the role You have ordained for him.

His Side

> A righteous man is cautious in friendship, but the way of the wicked leads them astray. *Proverbs 12:26*

Lord, make my husband cautious about who he chooses for his best friends. While he is called to be salt and light in the world and to befriend the lost as Christ did, bring him godly men with whom he can form strong bonds—men who will influence him to follow You more closely, love You more deeply, and listen to You more carefully.

His Sexuality

> But among you there must not be even a hint of sexual immorality, or of any kind of impurity, or of greed, because these are improper for God's holy people. *Ephesians 5:3*

Enable and empower my husband to not allow even a hint of sexual immorality or impurity in his thoughts or actions. Help him remember that You have set him apart for Your holy purposes.

His Legs

Now it is God who makes both us and you stand firm in Christ. He anointed us, set his seal of ownership on us, and put his Spirit in our hearts as a deposit, guaranteeing what is to come. *2 Corinthians 1:21–22*

Embolden my husband with Your strength so that he will not waver in his beliefs but stand firm in his faith. Thank You for setting your seal of ownership on him and putting Your Holy Spirit in him as a deposit guaranteeing what is to come.

His Knees

Submit yourselves, then, to God. *James 4:7*

May my husband submit to Your authority and Your will today. Give him a humble and yielding spirit so that he will make You the Commander in Chief of his life.

His Feet

This is what the LORD says: "Stand at the crossroads and look; ask for the ancient paths, ask where the good way is, and walk in it, and you will find rest for your souls." *Jeremiah 6:16*

As my husband stands at various crossroads today—places where he has to decide whether to turn to the left or right—open his eyes to see the footprints of godly men and women who have gone before him. Give him the humility to ask for direction and the wisdom to walk on the right path. Help him discover the rest for his soul that comes from trusting that Your way is the best way. In Jesus' name, amen.

Day Twenty-Four

His Mind

> For this reason, since the day we heard about you, we have not stopped praying for you and asking God to fill you with the knowledge of his will through all spiritual wisdom and understanding. *Colossians 1:9*

Dear Lord, I pray You will fill my husband's mind with the knowledge of Your will. Give him spiritual wisdom and understanding that go beyond human explanation and earthly education. Help him understand the truths of Scripture like never before.

His Eyes

> As they talked and discussed these things with each other, Jesus himself came up and walked along with them; but they were kept from recognizing him.... Then their eyes were opened and they recognized him, and he disappeared from their sight. *Luke 24:15–16, 31*

Lord, open my husband's eyes so that he will recognize Your presence and Your work in his life today. Please don't let him move through his day unaware, but heighten his sensitivity to Your glory all around.

His Ears

> In the morning, O Lord, you hear my voice; in the morning
> I lay my requests before you and wait in expectation.
> *Psalm 5:3*

Lord, as my husband lays his requests and petitions before You each morning, teach him how to recognize Your voice and expect You to speak.

His Mouth

> Without wood a fire goes out;
> without gossip a quarrel dies down.
> *Proverbs 26:20*

Keep my husband from throwing wood on the fires of anger and contention with gossip or divisive chatter. Instead, help him smother the flames of quarrels with a blanket of silence.

His Neck

> Therefore do not be foolish, but understand what the Lord's will is.
> *Ephesians 5:17*

Protect my husband from being foolish or careless in his decision-making process. Give him understanding so that he may clearly comprehend what You want him to do and how You want him to do it.

His Shoulders

> Peace I leave with you; my peace I give you. I do not give to you as the
> world gives. Do not let your hearts be troubled and do not be afraid.
> *John 14:27*

I pray my husband will not be troubled or afraid of the future but filled with the peace only Your Son, Jesus, can give. Keep him from being agitated or anxious about the burdens of this world. Let him be calm and assured by trusting the promises of Your Word.

His Heart

> And the peace of God, which transcends all understanding,
> will guard your hearts and your minds in Christ Jesus.
> *Philippians 4:7*

Thank You, God, for the gift of Your peace, which transcends all under-standing. May it guard and protect my husband's heart. I ask You to keep his heart under the surveillance of Your all-seeing eyes and behind the fortress of Your protective care.

His Back

You hem me in—behind and before;

you have laid your hand upon me.

Psalm 139:5

Almighty God, hem my husband in today. Be a shield behind him and before him. May Your hand be upon him to guard his every step. Thank You for the assurance that there is no place he can go that is out of Your protective reach. I pray You will have his back today.

His Arms

But he said to me, "My grace is sufficient for you, for my power is made perfect in weakness." Therefore I will boast all the more gladly about my weaknesses, so that Christ's power may rest on me.... For when I am weak, then I am strong. *2 Corinthians 12:9–10*

When my husband feels weak in any area of his life, help him remember that Your grace is sufficient—that Your strength is enough to get him through any struggle, over any mountain, around any roadblock. May he see his weakness as the perfect backdrop for Your glorious power and might to be displayed in his life.

His Hands

Whatever you do, work at it with all your heart, as working for the Lord, not for men. *Colossians 3:23*

Whatever tasks my husband performs today, encourage him to work with all his heart, as working for You and not for men. Help him to work as if his paycheck and his bonus were coming directly from You.

His Ring Finger

Husbands, love your wives, just as Christ loved the church and gave himself up for her to make her holy, cleansing her by the washing with water through the word, and to present her to himself as a radiant church, without stain or wrinkle or any other blemish, but holy and blameless. *Ephesians 5:25–27*

Lord, show my husband how to love me just as Christ loved the Church and gave Himself up for her. Teach him how to be a sanctifying agent in my life, helping me to be more and more like Jesus every day. And, Lord, help me embrace the process and not be resistant to it. Help me be an easy woman to love.

His Side

Bear with each other and forgive whatever grievances you may have against one another. Forgive as the Lord forgave you. *Colossians 3:13*

Please help my husband be kind and compassionate in all his relationships. Stir him to forgive others quickly and completely, just as You have forgiven him. I pray he will not hold a grudge or plan revenge but will let go the offenses and let You take care of the rest.

His Sexuality

Put to death, therefore, whatever belongs to your earthly nature: sexual immorality, impurity, lust, evil desires and greed, which is idolatry. *Colossians 3:5*

Give my husband the desire and the power to get rid of anything that belongs to his earthly nature: sexual immorality, impurity, lust, evil desires, greed, and idolatry. Help him honor sexual intimacy as a gift from You to be enjoyed by husband and wife.

His Legs

It is for freedom that Christ has set us free. Stand firm, then, and do not let yourselves be burdened again by a yoke of slavery. *Galatians 5:1*

Empower my husband to stand firm on the finished work of Jesus Christ. I pray he will live fully and free in Your mercy and grace. Keep him from being burdened by religious rules and regulations that have nothing to do with a relationship with You. Protect him from falling into the trap of trying to earn what he already has in You.

His Knees

Exalt the LORD our God! Bow low before his feet, for he is holy! *Psalm 99:5,* NLT

Put a passion in my husband to exalt You today. Stir him to bow before You in awe of Your holiness.

His Feet

When Jesus spoke again to the people, he said, "I am the light of the world. Whoever follows me will never walk in darkness, but will have the light of life." *John 8:12*

Guide my husband's feet today so that he will not walk in the darkness of this present world but in the light of Christ. Keep him from stumbling about in confusion or uncertainty, and illumine his path so that he can walk securely in the radiance of truth. In Jesus' name, amen.

Day Twenty-Five

His Mind

> Set your minds on things above, not on earthly things. *Colossians 3:2*

Heavenly Father, I pray my husband will set his mind on things above and not on earthly things. Keep his thought life rotating on the axis of eternal truth.

His Eyes

> For since the creation of the world God's invisible qualities—his eternal power and divine nature—have been clearly seen, being understood from what has been made, so that men are without excuse. *Romans 1:20*

Heavenly Father, open my husband's eyes to see Your invisible qualities, Your eternal power, and Your divine nature through what You have made. Don't let my husband miss the splendor of Your creation, but help him recognize Your glory as revealed through the works of Your hand.

His Ears

> He [Satan] was a murderer from the beginning. He has always hated the truth, because there is no truth in him. When he lies, it is consistent with his character; for he is a liar and the father of lies. *John 8:44,* NLT

Close my husband's ear to Satan's lies. Help him recognize Satan's lies quickly, reject Satan's lies completely, and replace Satan's lies with Your truth. Remind him that he doesn't have to out-muscle him or out-fight him but simply out-truth him.

His Mouth

Do not lie to each other, since you have taken off your old self with its practices. *Colossians 3:9*

Enable my husband to speak only what is truthful, no matter how difficult telling the truth may be or how enticing a tweak of the facts may seem.

His Neck

And pray in the Spirit on all occasions with all kinds of prayers and requests. *Ephesians 6:18*

When my husband has a decision to make, prompt him to bring it before You. Stir him to pray in the Spirit on all occasions with all kinds of prayers and requests.

His Shoulders

And the Holy Spirit helps us in our weakness. *Romans 8:26,* NLT

Lord, thank You for the Holy Spirit who helps us in our weakness. When my husband feels burdened or anxious today, urge him to call on the Holy Spirit who is there to lift the weight off his shoulders.

His Heart

Let the peace of Christ rule in your hearts, since as members of one body you were called to peace.
Colossians 3:15

I pray my husband will invite the peace of Christ to sit on the throne of his heart and rule his life today. May he strive to live in unity and peace with all believers as You have called him to do.

His Back

> So we say with confidence, "The Lord is my helper;
> I will not be afraid. What can mere mortals do to me?"
> *Hebrews 13:6,* NIV 2011

Keep my husband free from worry or fear about what mere mortals can do to him, and help him rest assured in the knowledge that You are his Helper, Defender, and Protector. Shield him from anyone who would seek to do him harm.

His Arms

> And we pray this in order that you may live a life worthy of the
> Lord and may please him in every way...being strengthened with
> all power according to his glorious might so that you may have
> great endurance and patience. *Colossians 1:10–11*

Lord, strengthen my husband with Your power according to Your glorious might. Give him great endurance and patience as he accesses the power of the Holy Spirit in him.

His Hands

> Make it your ambition to lead a quiet life, to mind your own
> business and to work with your hands, just as we told you,
> so that your daily life may win the respect of outsiders and
> so that you will not be dependent on anybody.
> *1 Thessalonians 4:11–12*

I pray my husband will make it his ambition to lead a quiet life, mind his own business, and work diligently at his own job so that his daily life may win the respect of those outside the Christian faith and so that he will not be dependent on anybody for financial assistance.

His Ring Finger

If you have any encouragement from being united with Christ, if any comfort from his love, if any fellowship with the Spirit, if any tenderness and compassion, then make my joy complete by being like-minded, having the same love, being one in spirit and purpose.
Philippians 2:1–2

Dear Lord, I pray my husband and I will be unified in Christ and like-minded in love. Bless us with a deep-seated friendship as well as deep-spirited love. Help us be one physically and spiritually, united by our common purpose of glorifying You in our marriage and in our lives. In Jesus' name, amen.

His Side

Do nothing out of selfish ambition or vain conceit, but in humility consider others better than yourselves. Each of you should look not only to your own interests, but also to the interests of others.
Philippians 2:3–4

Stir my husband to do nothing out of selfish ambition or vain conceit but to do everything with humility and grace. Keep him from simply looking out for his own interests, but prompt him to demonstrate concern for others, looking for ways to help them succeed and accomplish their dreams.

His Sexuality

Marriage should be honored by all, and the marriage bed kept pure, for God will judge the adulterer and all the sexually immoral. *Hebrews 13:4*

I pray my husband will honor our marriage and keep our marriage bed pure.

His Legs

> If sinners entice you, do not give in to them. *Proverbs 1:10*

If anyone tries to entice or tempt my husband to sin, give him the courage and confidence to stand firm in his faith and walk away.

His Knees

> You shall have no other gods before me. You shall not make for yourself an idol in the form of anything in heaven above or on the earth beneath or in the waters below. You shall not bow down to them or worship them; for I, the Lord your God, am a jealous God. *Exodus 20:3–5*

Help my husband to recognize and avoid any form of idolatry in his life. Give him the determination to not allow anyone or anything to take Your rightful place as Lord.

His Feet

> Therefore, being always of good courage, and knowing that while we are at home in the body we are absent from the Lord—for we walk by faith, not by sight. *2 Corinthians 5:6–7,* NASB

Empower and equip my husband to walk by faith and not by sight. Show him that there is more to this life than what he can see with his physical eyes. Help him to trust in, believe in, and cling to what he knows to be true in Your Word, even if what he sees in the world around him doesn't seem to line up with it. May faith in Your truth be his North Star as he navigates his day. In Jesus' name, amen.

Day Twenty-Six

His Mind

Let the word of Christ dwell in you richly. *Colossians 3:16*

Dear Lord, I pray that the Word of Christ will dwell in my husband richly. I pray he will not open the door for the Word of Christ to stop by for visits every now and then but invite Your Word to take up permanent residence in his mind.

His Eyes

See, I am doing a new thing! Now it springs up; do you not perceive it? I am making a way in the desert and streams in the wasteland. *Isaiah 43:19*

Open my husband's eyes to see how You are working in his life and providing for his needs. Make him alert to the streams You have placed in his desert and the roadways You have made in his wilderness. Don't let him get stuck in a rut of dull and predictable checklists, but help him live in watchful expectation for new and exciting plans You have for his life.

His Ears

The watchman opens the gate for him, and the sheep listen to his voice. He calls his own sheep by name and leads them out. When he has brought out all his own, he goes on ahead of them, and his sheep follow him because they know his voice. *John 10:3–4*

Jesus, thank You for shepherding my husband today. Thank You for going ahead of him and calling out to him. I pray he will recognize Your voice and follow where You lead.

His Mouth

Reckless words pierce like a sword, but the tongue of the wise brings healing. *Proverbs 12:18*

Keep my husband from speaking too quickly or recklessly. Help him to weigh his words carefully before they escape his lips. Show him how to speak healing into the lives of others, and give him the courage to do so.

His Neck

And this is my prayer: that your love may abound more and more in knowledge and depth of insight, so that you may be able to discern what is best and may be pure and blameless until the day of Christ. *Philippians 1:9–10*

I pray my husband's love for You will abound more and more in knowledge and depth of insight. Give him discernment to make the best choices and wisdom to live pure and blameless until Christ returns or You take him home.

His Shoulders

Now to him who is able to do immeasurably more than all we ask or imagine, according to his power that is at work within us, to him be glory in the church and in Christ Jesus throughout all generations, for ever and ever! *Ephesians 3:20–21*

Lord, whatever pressures my husband may face today, help him remember that You are able to do immeasurably more than all he asks or imagines. Prompt him to cling to the truth that You can accomplish more through a willing servant in one day than a self-sufficient man can accomplish in a lifetime.

His Heart

Hope deferred makes the heart sick, but a longing fulfilled is
a tree of life. *Proverbs 13:12*

Protect my husband from losing hope and becoming heartsick. Bolster
his faith so that he will not give up but press on toward accomplish-
ing all You have called him to do. May he not be a sapling languish-
ing in self-sufficiency but a mighty oak planted by the streams of living
water.

His Back

When you pass through the waters, I will be with you; and when you
pass through the rivers, they will not sweep over you. When you walk
through the fire, you will not be burned; the flames will not set you
ablaze. *Isaiah 43:2*

When my husband passes through rough waters and feels as if he is in
over his head, save him from drowning and set his feet on dry ground.
When he walks through fiery trials and feels as if everything is about to
go up in flames, extinguish the blaze and keep him from harm. No matter what trials come his way today, remind him that You are with him to
protect and deliver him.

His Arms

This is what the Sovereign LORD, the Holy One of Israel, says:...
"In quietness and trust is your strength."
Isaiah 30:15

Keep my husband from scurrying about trying to do everything in his
own strength. Remind him to be still and trust in Your sovereign plan
and to draw from Your almighty power.

His Hands

> What he [the Holy One] opens no one can shut, and what he shuts no
> one can open. *Revelation 3:7*

Lord, I ask You to open doors in the workplace that would help my husband thrive and close doors that would hinder his progress. Keep him from trying to force something to happen that is not in Your perfect will. Give him the courage to act quickly when You have made a way or opened up an opportunity. Bless him with the discernment to know the difference.

His Ring Finger

> In this same way, husbands ought to love their wives as their own
> bodies. He who loves his wife loves himself.... Each one of you also
> must love his wife as he loves himself, and the wife must respect
> her husband. *Ephesians 5:28, 33*

Stir my husband's heart to love me as he loves his own body. Show him how to care for me and cherish me as half of his whole, remembering that when he takes care of me, he is taking care of a part of himself. Just as I desire to be loved and cherished, Your Word tells me that my husband longs to be respected. Help me to never disrespect him with my words or actions, knowing that when I honor him I honor You.

His Side

> Therefore, as God's chosen people, holy and dearly loved,
> clothe yourselves with compassion, kindness, humility,
> gentleness and patience. Bear with each other and forgive
> whatever grievances you may have against one another.
> Forgive as the Lord forgave you. And over all these virtues
> put on love, which binds them all together in perfect unity.
> *Colossians 3:12–14*

Dear Lord, since my husband is Your chosen, holy, and dearly loved child, I pray he will clothe himself in the outfit You have picked out for him: compassion, kindness, gentleness, and patience. Help him to bear with the quirks of people who rub him the wrong way and to forgive as quickly and completely as You have forgiven him. Most of all, I pray that he will put on and wear love as his basic, all-purpose garment, never leaving home without it.

His Sexuality

> Blessed is the man who endures temptation; for when he has been approved, he will receive the crown of life which the Lord has promised to those who love Him. *James 1:12,* NKJV

Empower my husband to endure sexual temptation and not fall prey to the devil's enticing tactics. If he is tested in this area, enable him to pass with flying colors and be blessed with the reward of Your approval.

His Legs

> Put on the full armor of God so that you can take your stand against the devil's schemes. *Ephesians 6:11*

Please don't allow my husband to be caught off guard or unprepared for the devil's schemes. Keep him fully alert and completely protected so that he can stand unwavering against any assault.

His Knees

> He guides the humble in what is right and teaches them his way. *Psalm 25:9*

Lord, keep my husband from being proud and mistakenly believing he can handle life on his own. Instead, prompt him to humble himself before You, learn from You, and live for You.

His Feet

But I say, walk by the Spirit, and you will not carry out the desire of the flesh. *Galatians 5:16,* NASB

I pray my husband will not walk according to the flesh, attempting to get his needs met apart from Christ, but that he will walk according to the Spirit, obeying You in all he does. Guide his steps. Illumine his path. Make the way clear. In Jesus' name, amen.

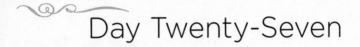

Day Twenty-Seven

His Mind

> For God has not given us a spirit of fear, but of power and of love and
> of a sound mind. *2 Timothy 1:7,* NKJV

Lord, give my husband a sound mind today. Help him have clear, concise, and controlled thinking. Protect him from any spirit of confusion that would attempt to cloud his thinking or jumble his thoughts.

His Eyes

> So we fix our eyes not on what is seen, but on what is unseen. For what
> is seen is temporary, but what is unseen is eternal. *2 Corinthians 4:18*

Guide my husband to fix his eyes not on what is seen and temporary, such as people, possessions, or position, but on what is unseen and eternal, such as spiritual blessings in the here and now—and everlasting life in the world to come.

His Ears

> Obscene stories, foolish talk, and coarse jokes—these are not for you.
> *Ephesians 5:4,* NLT

Prompt my husband to walk away from obscene stories, foolish talk, and coarse jokes. May he refuse to listen to conversations that are unworthy of his attention. Keep him from allowing impure thoughts to enter his mind through what he listens to today.

His Mouth

> Be wise in the way you act toward outsiders; make the most of every
> opportunity. *Colossians 4:5*

Make my husband particularly sensitive to the words he speaks when he is around those who don't know You as Savior and Lord. Teach him how to make the most of every opportunity to be Your spokesman in the world.

His Neck

> Do not be anxious about anything, but in everything,
> by prayer and petition, with thanksgiving, present your
> requests to God. *Philippians 4:6*

When my husband has a decision to make, I pray he will not be anxious about it but pray about it. Prompt him to present his prayers and petitions to You, thanking You in advance for the answer that is sure to come.

His Shoulders

> Do not be anxious about anything, but in everything, by prayer and
> petition, with thanksgiving, present your requests to God. And the
> peace of God, which transcends all understanding, will guard your
> hearts and your minds in Christ Jesus. *Philippians 4:6–7*

When my husband feels weighed down by the cares of this world, I pray he will cut the burden off his shoulders with the saber of prayer and tie it on Your shoulders with the cords of praise. May Your peace, which transcends all human understanding, guard his heart and his mind so that he will not pick up those burdens and start worrying again.

His Heart

> Since, then, you have been raised with Christ, set your hearts on
> things above, where Christ is seated at the right hand of God.
> *Colossians 3:1*

Teach my husband to set his heart on things above, rather than on earthly things. May he desire the eternal treasures of Your kingdom above the temporary rewards of this world.

His Back

Holy Father, protect them by the power of your name—the name you gave me—so that they may be one as we are one.... My prayer is not that you take them out of the world but that you protect them from the evil one. *John 17:11, 15*

I am so thankful that, just as Jesus prayed for His disciples, He now speaks to You on behalf of my husband (Romans 8:34). I join Jesus in asking You to protect my husband from the Evil One by the power of Your name.

His Arms

I pray that from his glorious, unlimited resources he [God] will empower you with inner strength through his Spirit. *Ephesians 3:16,* NLT

Almighty God, endow my husband with inner strength through the power of the Holy Spirit. Equip him and fortify him from the glorious, unlimited resources of heaven.

His Hands

Do not wear yourself out to get rich; have the wisdom to show restraint. Cast but a glance at riches, and they are gone, for they will surely sprout wings and fly off to the sky like an eagle. *Proverbs 23:4–5*

In a world obsessed with obtaining wealth, I pray my husband will set healthy boundaries and priorities. I pray he will not spend his life working to accumulate riches that can so easily sprout wings and fly away but invest his life in faith, family, and friends. I ask You to grant him success and satisfaction and to help him resist an unhealthy craving for more.

His Ring Finger

Give honor to marriage, and remain faithful to one another in marriage. *Hebrews 13:4,* NLT

Give my husband and me an undeniable, unwavering commitment to honor our marriage vows and remain faithful to one another even when life doesn't go according to plan.

His Side

Make every effort to live in peace with all men. *Hebrews 12:14*

Loving Father, move my husband to make every effort to live in peace with all men. Show him how to settle every conflict quickly and peacefully, and then give him the courage to do so.

His Sexuality

When tempted, no one should say, "God is tempting me." For God cannot be tempted by evil, nor does he tempt anyone; but each one is tempted when, by his own evil desire, he is dragged away and enticed. Then, after desire has conceived, it gives birth to sin; and sin, when it is full-grown, gives birth to death. *James 1:13–15*

Father, protect my husband so that he will not fall into temptation or be dragged away and enticed by evil desires. Strengthen him to resist the lure of sexual temptation and to run away from sexual sin. When temptation knocks at the door, I pray he will not open it or even look through the peephole to catch a quick glimpse.

His Legs

> For our struggle is not against flesh and blood, but against
> the rulers, against the authorities, against the powers of this
> dark world and against the spiritual forces of evil in the
> heavenly realms. Therefore put on the full armor of God,
> so that when the day of evil comes, you may be able to stand
> your ground, and after you have done everything, to stand.
>
> *Ephesians 6:12–13*

Father God, remind my husband that his struggle is not against flesh and blood (mere human beings) but against the rulers, against the authorities, against the powers of this dark world, and against the spiritual forces of evil in the heavenly realms. Prompt him to put on the full armor of God from head to toe, so that when the Evil One attacks, he will have done everything possible to stand firm. Empower him to take his stand and not allow the Enemy one inch of conquered ground.

His Knees

> Very early in the morning, while it was still dark, Jesus got up,
> left the house and went off to a solitary place, where he prayed.
>
> *Mark 1:35*

Lord, I entreat You to make my husband a man of prayer. Just as Jesus rose early in the morning to spend time alone with You, put a desire in my husband to take time during his busy day to get alone with You. I ask that prayer will not be something he feels he *has* to do but something he feels he *gets* to do. Oh Lord, make my husband a man of prayer.

His Feet

> Therefore, since we are surrounded by such a great cloud of
> witnesses, let us throw off everything that hinders and the sin

that so easily entangles. And let us run with perseverance the race marked out for us, fixing our eyes on Jesus, the pioneer and perfecter of faith. *Hebrews 12:1–2,* NIV 2011

Teach my husband how to throw off everything that hinders him from running well the great race of life. Convict him to strip off any sin that would tangle up his feet, slow him down, or trip him up. Give him the stamina to run with perseverance the race You have marked out for him and not worry about the race that You have marked out for someone else. Keep his eyes fixed on the goal of becoming more and more like Christ every day, and keep his feet on the right path to do so. In Jesus' name, amen.

Day Twenty-Eight

His Mind

> Therefore, holy brothers, who share in the heavenly calling, fix your thoughts on Jesus, the apostle and high priest whom we confess.
>
> *Hebrews 3:1*

Dear Lord, I pray my husband will fix his thoughts on Jesus today. May he make Jesus the centerpiece of everything he believes and thinks. Even though the world, the flesh, and the devil will bombard him with distractions on every side, I pray he will secure his mind on Jesus.

His Eyes

> Holy, holy, holy is the LORD Almighty; the whole earth is full of his glory. *Isaiah 6:3*

Open my husband's eyes to see Your glory all around. Help him notice Your handiwork in the small and the large, the minutia of an insect and the grandness of the night sky. Help him to pay attention so that he won't miss Your fingerprints throughout the day.

His Ears

> Let no one deceive you with empty words, for because of these things the wrath of God comes upon the sons of disobedience.
>
> *Ephesians 5:6,* NKJV

Lord, keep my husband from listening to or being deceived by foolish talk of empty-headed men or slick sales pitches of the worldly wise. Give him discernment to identify and resist empty words, big promises, and persuasive arguments that could lead him astray.

His Mouth

> Let your conversation be always full of grace, seasoned
> with salt, so that you may know how to answer everyone.
> *Colossians 4:6*

Father, teach my husband how to speak words that are full of grace and seasoned with salt, words that make others thirsty to know You more. Help him to use speech that represents You well.

His Neck

> If you need wisdom, ask our generous God, and he
> will give it to you. He will not rebuke you for asking.
> *James 1:5,* NLT

When my husband has a decision to make, give him wisdom, understanding, and discernment. Keep him from depending on his own logic, and prompt him to ask You for supernatural insight.

His Shoulders

> I have learned the secret of being content in any and every
> situation, whether well fed or hungry, whether living in plenty
> or in want. I can do everything through him who gives me
> strength. *Philippians 4:12–13*

Sovereign Lord, show my husband how to be content in any and every circumstance. Deliver him from the culture's mantra of "More is better," and teach him to be satisfied with what he has. Help me not to add to his load by complaining, grumbling, or wanting more material possessions. May we both learn the secret to contentment: whatever we have, wherever we are, we can do all things through Christ who gives us strength.

His Heart

> May he strengthen your hearts so that you will be blameless and holy
> in the presence of our God and Father when our Lord Jesus comes
> with all his holy ones. *1 Thessalonians 3:13*

Lord, strengthen my husband's heart with righteous resolve and pure conviction so that he will be blameless and holy in Your presence. Fortify his heart with confident faith so that if Jesus were to return today, he would not be ashamed.

His Back

> And having disarmed the powers and authorities, he made a public
> spectacle of them, triumphing over them by the cross. *Colossians 2:15*

Lord, I stand on the promise that the devil has no authority over my husband because You have disarmed the spiritual powers and authorities of evil, made a public spectacle of them in the heavenlies, and triumphed over them by the Cross. I pray You will protect my husband from the Enemy's attempt to retake any conquered ground. I praise You for the assurance that greater is Jesus who reigns in my husband than the defeated devil that is in the world (1 John 4:4).

His Arms

> His divine power has given us everything we need for life and godliness
> through our knowledge of him who called us by his own glory and
> goodness. *2 Peter 1:3*

When my husband feels too weak to meet the challenges of life, infuse him with Your power and Your strength. Assure him that You have given him everything he needs for life and godliness through his knowledge of Jesus who called him by His own glory and goodness. Move him to plug into Your power and access Your strength.

His Hands

No one can serve two masters. Either he will hate the one
and love the other, or he will be devoted to the one and
despise the other. You cannot serve both God and Money.
Matthew 6:24

Help my husband to not place too much importance on making money.
Show him how to master his money so that his money does not master him. Keep him from working to simply accumulate worldly riches,
and encourage him to be diligent to glorify You. Guide him not to
work too little and become lazy, and not to work too much and become obsessed.

His Ring Finger

Husbands, in the same way be considerate as you live with your wives,
and treat them with respect as the weaker partner and as heirs with
you of the gracious gift of life, so that nothing will hinder your prayers.
1 Peter 3:7

Enable my husband to be considerate of me, respectful toward me, and
gentle with me so that nothing will hinder his prayers. Thank You, Lord,
that even though I may be weaker physically, my husband and I are spiritually equal coheirs of Christ.

His Side

Therefore encourage one another and build each other up, just as in
fact you are doing. *1 Thessalonians 5:11*

Loving Lord, make my husband an encourager in all his relationships.
Show him how to build others up and not tear them down. Teach him
how to fan the flames of enthusiasm and not quench the embers of
excitement.

His Sexuality

> It is God's will that you should be sanctified: that you
> should avoid sexual immorality; that each of you should
> learn to control his own body in a way that is holy and
> honorable, not in passionate lust like the heathen, who
> do not know God. *1 Thessalonians 4:3–5*

Holy Father, remind my husband that he is set apart for pure and godly living. Help him avoid all sexual immorality, controlling his own body in a way that is holy and honorable. Prompt him to be on guard at all times, refusing to look at, listen to, or engage in any activity that would tempt him sexually.

His Legs

> It is by faith you stand firm. *2 Corinthians 1:24*

Lord, give my husband a strong faith that does not waver. Help him to stand firm in his convictions and strong in his beliefs.

His Knees

> Draw near to God and He will draw near to you. *James 4:8,* NASB

I pray my husband will start his day in communion with You, continue his day in union with You, and end his day with thanksgiving to You. Thank You for drawing near to him.

His Feet

> If we claim to have fellowship with him yet walk in the darkness, we lie
> and do not live by the truth. But if we walk in the light, as he is in the
> light, we have fellowship with one another, and the blood of Jesus, his
> Son, purifies us from all sin. *1 John 1:6–7*

Sovereign Lord, I pray that You will keep my husband from walking in the darkness of the world, the flesh, or the devil. Instead, guide him to always walk in the light of Christ with other believers. I pray all this in Jesus' name, amen.

Day Twenty-Nine

His Mind

> If any of you lacks wisdom, he should ask God, who gives generously to all without finding fault, and it will be given to him. But when he asks, he must believe and not doubt, because he who doubts is like a wave of the sea, blown and tossed by the wind. That man should not think he will receive anything from the Lord; he is a double-minded man, unstable in all he does. *James 1:5–8*

I pray my husband will not be double-minded in any way. May his thoughts not be tossed about like a toy boat on a stormy sea, wavering between belief and doubt, trust and worry, peace and anxiety, but glide like a steady ship on quiet waters of trusting faith.

His Eyes

> Be self-controlled and alert. Your enemy the devil prowls around like a roaring lion looking for someone to devour. *1 Peter 5:8*

Lord, prompt my husband to pay attention to what he looks at today. Keep him alert to the devil's tempting tactics to draw his eyes to sin. Empower him to have restraint and show self-control by turning his eyes away from temptation, and thus escape the Enemy's trap.

His Ears

> For the time will come when men will not put up with sound doctrine. Instead, to suit their own desires, they will gather around them a great number of teachers to say what their itching ears want to hear. They will turn their ears away from the truth and turn aside to myths. *2 Timothy 4:3–4*

Lord Most High, shut my husband's ears to those who distort the truth. Keep him from listening to teachers who twist Scripture to suit man's agendas and desires, and move him to pay attention to teachers who declare the full gospel of Jesus Christ. May he refuse to listen to men whose idea of right and wrong changes with the seasons but eagerly listen to sound doctrine that remains the same yesterday, today, and forever.

His Mouth

Everyone should be quick to listen, slow to speak and slow to become angry. *James 1:19*

I pray my husband will be quick to listen, slow to speak, and slow to become angry. I pray he will lead with his ears and follow with his mouth.

His Neck

But in their distress they turned to the LORD, the God of Israel, and sought him, and he was found by them. *2 Chronicles 15:4*

Lord, urge my husband to turn to You in times of distress. Prompt him to seek Your will in every decision he makes.

His Shoulders

And my God will meet all your needs according to his glorious riches in Christ Jesus. *Philippians 4:19*

All-Sufficient God, help my husband trust that You will supply all his needs according to Your glorious riches in Christ Jesus. Take away his burdens and worries and replace them with confidence and peace.

His Heart

But I say, love your enemies! Pray for those who persecute you! *Matthew 5:44,* NLT

Lord, soften my husband's heart to love his enemies and pray for those who persecute him. Protect his heart from becoming bitter or resentful, and fill his heart with mercy and grace.

His Back

But the Lord is faithful, and he will strengthen and protect you from the evil one. *2 Thessalonians 3:3*

Faithful Father, strengthen my husband and protect him from the Evil One. Help him to be alert to the devil's schemes and attentive to the Enemy's attempts to trip him up.

His Arms

Finally, be strong in the Lord and in his mighty power. *Ephesians 6:10*

Omnipotent God, make my husband strong in You and in Your mighty power. Give him the strength to do all You have called him to do today.

His Hands

[Jesus said to the disciples,] "Come with me by yourselves to a quiet place and get some rest." *Mark 6:31*

Father, please help my husband know when to stop working and get some rest. Prompt him to pull away from everyone and everything in order to spend quiet time with You. Show me how to make space and opportunity for my husband to relax, recharge, and refresh.

His Ring Finger

Now the serpent was more crafty than any of the wild animals the LORD God had made. He said to the woman, "Did God really say, 'You must not eat from any tree in the garden'?" *Genesis 3:1*

Just as Satan slithered into the Garden of Eden to cause distrust, discord, and disunity in the very first marriage, he continues to prowl around looking for marriages to destroy today. Help my husband and me detect the Enemy's destructive tactics quickly and defeat his attempts to destroy us completely. Teach us how to beat back the Enemy with Your Word and prayer. Place Your hedge of protection around our marriage.

His Side

Two are better than one, because they have a good return for their work: If one falls down, his friend can help him up. But pity the man who falls and has no one to help him up!
Ecclesiastes 4:9–10

Lord, please give my husband at least one godly friend who will help him up when he falls. Make him a man who will not desert his friends when they fall but help them get back up again.

His Sexuality

For God did not call us to be impure, but to live a holy life. Therefore, he who rejects this instruction does not reject man but God, who gives you his Holy Spirit. *1 Thessalonians 4:7–8*

Father, give my husband the desire, the determination, and the power to lead a sexually pure and holy life. I pray he will not reject You by rejecting sexual purity but honor You by embracing a holy lifestyle.

His Legs

He [Epaphras] is always wrestling in prayer for you, that you may stand firm in all the will of God, mature and fully assured.
Colossians 4:12

Empower my husband to stand firm in Your will, mature and fully assured. Make him a man of strong character and clear convictions. Help him to stand secure in a shaky world.

His Knees

Humble yourselves before the Lord, and he will lift you up. *James 4:10*

I pray that my husband will humble himself before You and that You will lift him up at the appointed time. Remind him that when he gets down on his knees before You, You will set him firmly on his feet.

His Feet

And this is love: that we walk in obedience to his commands. As you have heard from the beginning, his command is that you walk in love.
2 John v. 6

Lord, put a desire and determination in my husband's heart to walk in obedience to Your commands. I pray his steps will be guided by and motivated by his love for You and for others. In Jesus' name, amen.

Day Thirty

His Mind

> But solid food is for the mature, who by constant use have trained
> themselves to distinguish good from evil. *Hebrews 5:14*

Almighty God, I pray my husband will crave the solid food of Your Word.
May he not be satisfied with spoon-feeding by pastors and teachers but
take up fork and knife to dig into the meat of the Scriptures on his own. I
pray he will not be content with the knowledge he already has but will
hunger for the deeper truths of Scripture.

His Eyes

> Immediately, something like scales fell from Saul's eyes, and he could
> see again. *Acts 9:18*

Just as You removed the scales from Saul's eyes, I pray You will remove
any scales that prevent my husband from seeing You clearly. Open his
eyes. Help him see.

His Ears

> Blessed are your eyes because they see, and your ears because they
> hear. *Matthew 13:16*

Lord, reveal to my husband that he is most blessed when he opens his eyes
to see You and ears to hear You. Help him to be a man who listens to You.

His Mouth

> Avoid godless chatter, because those who indulge in it will become
> more and more ungodly. *2 Timothy 2:16*

Lord, prompt my husband to avoid godless chatter that could lead his heart away from You. May he not participate in or contribute to conversations that are not fitting for a follower of Christ.

His Neck

Solid food is for those who are mature, who through training have the skill to recognize the difference between right and wrong.

Hebrews 5:14, NLT

I pray that my husband will not only pull up to Your banqueting table and feast on the solid meat of Your Word but will also put what he learns into practice. Teach him how to discern what is right and wrong, good and evil, better and best.

His Shoulders

Cast all your anxiety on him because he cares for you.

1 Peter 5:7

Loving Lord, give my husband the wisdom and the will to cast all his anxieties on You once and for all. May he know without a shadow of a doubt that You care for his every need.

His Heart

For the love of money is a root of all kinds of evil. Some people, eager for money, have wandered from the faith and pierced themselves with many griefs. *1 Timothy 6:10*

While money is not evil in itself, Your Word tells us that the *love* of money is a root of all kinds of evil. I pray my husband will never let his desire to earn money or obtain wealth come before his desire to please You, serve You, and love You with all his heart.

His Back

> We know that God's children do not make a practice of sinning, for
> God's Son holds them securely, and the evil one cannot touch them.
> *1 John 5:18*, NLT

Heavenly Father, thank You for the assurance that Jesus carefully watches over and protects my husband. Thank You that Christ's divine presence holds him securely. Thank You that the devil cannot touch him. Thank You that nothing and no one can snatch him out of Your hand (John 10:29). I lay claim to those promises of protection for my husband today.

His Arms

> We also pray that you will be strengthened with all his glorious
> power so you will have all the endurance and patience you need.
> *Colossians 1:11*, NLT

Almighty God, strengthen my husband with power according to Christ's glorious might so that he may have supernatural endurance and patience in every difficult circumstance. Give him the stamina and fortitude he needs to complete every task You have called him to do.

His Hands

> Lazy people want much but get little, but those who work hard
> will prosper. *Proverbs 13:4*, NLT

Lord, instruct my husband to not be a lazy man who wants much and gets little but a hard worker who prospers and is rewarded for his labor. Help him to set healthy boundaries and goals. Keep him from being slothful or a workaholic, and show him proper balance of work and play.

His Ring Finger

Husbands, love your wives and do not be harsh with them.

Colossians 3:19

Heavenly Father, teach my husband and me how to love each other as You intended. Help us to not be harsh or bitter toward each other but gentle, forgiving, and kind.

His Side

Finally, all of you, be like-minded, be sympathetic, love one another, be compassionate and humble. *1 Peter 3:8,* NIV 2011

Show my husband how to love others as Christ has loved him—sacrificially and unconditionally. Encourage and empower him to be sympathetic, compassionate, and humble in his dealings with friends, family, and coworkers.

His Sexuality

If we confess our sins, He is faithful and just to forgive us our sins and to cleanse us from all unrighteousness. *1 John 1:9,* NKJV

If my husband has any sexual sin in his life, I pray he will confess it to You and receive forgiveness from You. Help him embrace Your grace and forgiveness and not limp about with the shackles of shame dangling from his ankles or the chains of guilt hanging around his neck. I pray he will live like a man set free and not a prisoner on parole.

His Legs

So then, brothers, stand firm and hold to the teachings we passed on to you, whether by word of mouth or by letter.

2 Thessalonians 2:15

Strengthen my husband with the power of the Holy Spirit so that he can stand firm on the truth of Jesus Christ and the teachings in Your Word. Protect him from faltering in his faith, wavering in his convictions, or allowing anyone or anything to weaken his stance.

His Knees

The prayer of a righteous man is powerful and effective. *James 5:16*

Devote yourselves to prayer, being watchful and thankful.

Colossians 4:2

I pray my husband will be a righteous man whose prayers are powerful and effective. Teach him to be devoted to prayer, watchful for Your responses, and thankful for Your answers.

His Feet

To him who is able to keep you from falling and to present you before his glorious presence without fault and with great joy— to the only God our Savior be glory, majesty, power and authority, through Jesus Christ our Lord, before all ages, now and forevermore! Amen. *Jude v. 24–25*

Finally, I praise You, Lord, because You are able to keep my husband from falling. I pray You will keep him standing on his feet without slipping or sliding into sin. I pray You will present my husband before Your glorious presence without fault and with great joy. To the only God our Savior be glory, majesty, power, and authority, through Jesus Christ our Lord, before all ages, now and forevermore! In Jesus' name, amen.

Appendix

I'd like to provide you with additional resources to cover your husband from head to toe regarding three vital areas that may be concerns in his life: his fatherhood if he is a dad, his salvation if he is not yet saved, and his healing if he is sick. I've crafted prayers for ten scriptures in each of these three areas, and if your husband fits into one of these categories, I encourage you to pray these over him often. Remember, "The prayer of a righteous person is powerful and effective" (James 5:16, NIV 2011).

Praying for His Salvation

s I mentioned in the opening chapter, there is no greater burden for a woman than for her unsaved husband and children to come to know Jesus as Savior and Lord. All else pales in the light of where they will spend eternity. Throughout this book I have encouraged you to pray for your husband as if he were already a Christian—calling things that are not as though they were—by faith (Romans 4:17). But if your husband has not yet made a decision to follow Christ, the following prayers are specifically designed for you to intercede for his salvation.

Prayer has mighty power to prepare the heart for the precious seed of truth to be planted. Prayer has supernatural strength to demolish strongholds of the Enemy that hold the sinner captive. Prayer has the potential to speak to the mountain of unbelief and cast it into the sea.

Remember, when you pray the Word of God, you pray the will of God. And God does not want anyone to perish but everyone to come to repentance (2 Peter 3:9).

Jesus looked at them and said, "With man this is impossible, but not with God; all things are possible with God." *Mark 10:27*

Lord, I am so thankful that nothing is impossible for You, no matter how bleak the situation may seem. I pray my husband will come to know Jesus as Savior and Lord. I place him into Your hands and wait with eager expectation for the day he says yes to You.

> He [Jesus] told them, "The harvest is plentiful, but the workers are few. Ask the Lord of the harvest, therefore, to send out workers into his harvest field." *Luke 10:2*

Heavenly Father, I ask that You send people into my husband's life to till the soil of his heart, to plant the seeds of truth, to water his parched soul with prayer, and to bring in the harvest. Just as You sent Philip to the Ethiopian seeker (Acts 8:27–30), Peter to the Samaritan sorcerer (Acts 8:9–25), and Paul to the businesswoman in Philippi (Acts 16:11–15), please place people in my husband's path who will point him toward You.

> But God demonstrates his own love for us in this: While we were still sinners, Christ died for us. *Romans 5:8*

Gracious God, please open my husband's eyes and heart to the truth that You have demonstrated Your love for him by sending Your Son to die for him. Let him know that he doesn't have to get his life tidied up before he comes to You but that You accept him just as he is, mess and all.

> For God so loved the world that he gave his one and only Son, that whoever believes in him shall not perish but have eternal life. *John 3:16*
>> For the Son of Man came to seek and to save what was lost. *Luke 19:10*

Lord, thank You for loving my husband so much that You gave Your one and only Son as a sacrifice for his sin. Thank You for Jesus' willingness to take on the form of human flesh and die on Calvary's cross. Thank You that Jesus came to seek and to save my husband. I pray my husband will turn from his sin and to You. Move his heart to believe on the Lord Jesus and be saved.

> [Jesus said,] "The thief comes only to steal and kill and destroy; I came that they may have life, and have it abundantly." *John 10:10,* NASB
>
> The reason the Son of God appeared was to destroy the devil's work. *1 John 3:8*

Deliver my husband from the powers of darkness that seek to steal and kill and destroy him by blinding his eyes to the truth and binding his heart to the lies. Release the Holy Spirit to thwart the Enemy's tactics, destroy the Enemy's strongholds, and render the Enemy impotent. I pray, almighty God, that You will destroy the devil's work in my husband's life—that You will tear down the walls, cut loose the shackles, and illuminate the darkness. Break my husband's pride. Humble him to bend his knees and raise a white flag of surrender to You. May he come to saving faith in Jesus and experience abundant life on earth and eternal life hereafter.

> [Jesus said,] "I tell you the truth, whoever hears my word and believes him who sent me has eternal life and will not be condemned; he has crossed over from death to life." *John 5:24*

I pray my husband will hear the Word of Truth and believe in Christ. May You break up the fallow ground of his heart and prepare the soil to receive Your Word. Put an urgency in his spirit regarding the importance of crossing over from spiritual death to eternal life. Stir up a desire in him to be born again. Remove any barriers that keep him from opening his heart and mind to You. Move him to believe on the Lord Jesus, receive eternal life, and be saved from the condemnation of hell. Please rescue him from the dominion of darkness and deliver him to the kingdom of Christ (Colossians 1:13).

> If you confess with your mouth, "Jesus is Lord," and believe in your heart that God raised him from the dead, you will be saved. For it is

with your heart that you believe and are justified, and it is with your
mouth that you confess and are saved.... For, "Everyone who calls on
the name of the Lord will be saved." *Romans 10:9–10, 13*

God, please convict my husband of his need to confess with his mouth,
"Jesus is Lord," and believe in his heart that You raised Him from the
dead. I pray in faith that my husband will call on the name of the Lord
Jesus and will be saved.

And even if our gospel is veiled, it is veiled to those who are perishing.
The god of this age has blinded the minds of unbelievers, so that they
cannot see the light of the gospel of the glory of Christ, who is the
image of God. *2 Corinthians 4:3–4*

Lord, please remove the veil over my husband's eyes that keeps him from
seeing the truth. Remove the influence of the god of this age, who blinds
my husband's mind and keeps him from understanding the truth of the
gospel. I ask You to flip the switch, to illumine his mind, so that the truth
of the gospel becomes clear and he will see that You sent Jesus, Your Son,
to die on the cross for him. For him! Open his mind to Your truth and
his heart to Your love.

The Lord is not slow in keeping his promise, as some understand
slowness. He is patient with you, not wanting anyone to perish, but
everyone to come to repentance. *2 Peter 3:9*

God our Savior, who wants all men to be saved and to come to a
knowledge of the truth. *1 Timothy 2:3–4*

God, I believe "all" means "all." I understand that You do not want my
husband to perish but to come to saving faith. I know that You do not
want my husband to spend eternity in hell separated from You but in
heaven rejoicing in Your presence. I pray You will do whatever is needed

in my husband's life to bring him to saving faith. I'm holding on and trusting You, fully persuaded that You will finish what You have started in him.

Here I am! I stand at the door and knock. If anyone hears my voice and opens the door, I will come in and eat with him, and he with me.

Revelation 3:20

Jesus, I pray my husband will sense You knocking on the door of his heart. Make him sensitive to Your persistent tapping and keenly aware of Your undeniable call so that he will no longer deny You access to all he is. I ask that You, as the loving and persistent "Hound of heaven," will nip at his heels until he stops running from You and starts running toward You. In Your name, I pray, amen.

Praying for His Fatherhood

Your husband will have many roles and responsibilities throughout his life, but none will be more important, more stressful, or more enjoyable than being a dad. President Theodore Roosevelt said it well: "No other success in life, not being President, or being wealthy, or going to college, or anything else, comes up to the success of the man and woman who can feel that they have done their duty and that their children and grandchildren rise up to call them blessed."[15]

God can give your husband clarity, confidence, and creative ideas to train up his children in the way they should go. So get down on your knees to pray for the children he will bounce on his!

Fix these words of mine in your hearts and minds; tie them as symbols on your hands and bind them on your foreheads. Teach them to your children, talking about them when you sit at home and when you walk along the road, when you lie down and when you get up. *Deuteronomy 11:18–19*

I pray my husband will fix Your Word in his heart and mind and get it deep inside his soul so that he can teach our children about Your principles, Your character, and Your ways. Give him a desire to make their faith training not just a Sunday morning activity but an everyday way of life.

Help him be a living example of godly character to our children from the time he gets up in the morning until he goes to bed at night.

> We will not hide these truths from our children; we will tell the next generation about the glorious deeds of the LORD, about his power and his mighty wonders.... So the next generation might know them—even the children not yet born—and they in turn will teach their own children. *Psalm 78:4, 6,* NLT

Put a desire and passion in my husband to tell our children about Your praiseworthy deeds and omnipotent power so that they will tell their children and they will tell their children. May my husband's godly influence be felt in generations yet to come, helping lead them to You.

> Train a child in the way he should go, and when he is old he will not turn from it. *Proverbs 22:6*

Give my husband the wisdom to know how to train up our children in the way they should go, trusting that when they are old, they will not turn from it. Help him teach by example and lead with love.

> My son, do not despise the LORD's discipline and do not resent his rebuke, because the LORD disciplines those he loves, as a father the son he delights in. *Proverbs 3:11–12*

Guide my husband so that he will not discipline our children too severely or too leniently. Give him the wisdom to know when to discipline and when to extend grace.

> Fathers, do not exasperate your children; instead, bring them up in the training and instruction of the Lord. *Ephesians 6:4*

Give my husband discernment and self-control, so that he will not provoke our children to anger or resentment by the way he treats them but rather bring them up with loving discipline and wise instruction that comes from You.

Jesus said to his disciples: "Things that cause people to stumble are bound to come, but woe to anyone through whom they come. It would be better for them to be thrown into the sea with a millstone tied around their neck than to cause one of these little ones to stumble." *Luke 17:1–2, NIV 2011*

Keep my husband from doing anything that would cause our children to stumble or fall into sin.

Do everything in love. *1 Corinthians 16:14*

Prompt my husband to sift everything he does to parent our children through the filter of love. Whether it is discipline, correction, or instruction, may love be the plumb line for his actions and words.

Remember this: Whoever sows sparingly will also reap sparingly, and whoever sows generously will also reap generously. *2 Corinthians 9:6*

Show my husband how to sow generously into the lives of our children. I pray he will not be stingy with his time, energy, or resources but will invest wisely in ways that will yield a bountiful harvest of godly character.

Fathers, do not embitter your children, or they will become discouraged. *Colossians 3:21*

Keep my husband from provoking, irritating, or embittering our children. Help him not to be too hard on them, lest they become discouraged or sullen or feel inferior. Give him wisdom to know how to discipline their stubbornness or rebelliousness without breaking their spirits.

Let us not become weary in doing good, for at the proper time we will reap a harvest if we do not give up. *Galatians 6:9*

When my husband feels tired and weary because he isn't seeing positive results from his parenting, encourage him to persevere. When he does not see good fruit he'd hoped for, encourage him to press on, knowing that he will reap a harvest at the proper time if he does not give up. In Jesus' name, amen.

Praying for His Healing

Illness or disease can bring the strongest man to his knees. Sickness is simply a part of living in a fallen world. Whether the sickness is an attack of the Enemy or a tool of our loving heavenly Father, we can pray for complete and total healing that brings glory to God.

As you pray for your husband's healing, please keep in mind that many times God uses sickness or disease to get someone's attention, to bring him to repentance, or to draw him into a more intimate relationship. He used leprosy to show Naaman he wasn't so powerful after all (2 Kings 5), a physical and psychological breakdown to humble haughty King Nebuchadnezzar (Daniel 4), a plague to halt a nation's rebellion (Numbers 16), and a nagging ailment to keep a powerful Paul on his knees (2 Corinthians 12:7).

And while we never want to interfere with God's work in the human heart, He does call us to pray. James instructs us, "Pray for each other so that you may be healed" (James 5:16). So we will pray.

As you pray for your husband's health, pray he will see God's hand in the healing process. When a crowd began praising Peter and John for the miraculous healing of a crippled beggar, Peter explained, "By faith in the name of Jesus, this man whom you see and know was made strong. It is Jesus' name and the faith that comes through him that has given this complete healing to him, as you can all see" (Acts 3:16). As one surgeon explained to me: "I make the cut. God heals the wound."

We are not praying for a life of comfort and ease but for one that is conformed to the image of Christ and framed in the sovereignty of God. We are called to pray in faith, believing. God is in charge of the outcome and the timing. The writer of Ecclesiastes reminds us, "[There is] a time to heal" (Ecclesiastes 3:3), and that time is when God says it's time.

But he was pierced for our transgressions, he was crushed for our iniquities; the punishment that brought us peace was upon him, and by his wounds we are healed. *Isaiah 53:5*

I pray that by Your stripes, my husband will be healed; by Your wounds, my husband would be made whole.

Praise the LORD, O my soul, and forget not all his benefits—who forgives all your sins and heals all your diseases, who redeems your life from the pit and crowns you with love and compassion, who satisfies your desires with good things so that your youth is renewed like the eagle's. *Psalm 103:2–5*

I praise You for being the God who heals all our diseases. I ask that You heal my husband, renew his strength, and restore his health.

Jesus went through all the towns and villages, teaching in their synagogues, preaching the good news of the kingdom and healing every disease and sickness. *Matthew 9:35*
Jesus Christ is the same yesterday and today and forever. *Hebrews 13:8*

Jesus, just as you went through all the towns and villages, healing every disease and sickness, I pray You will heal my husband. Just as You made the blind to see, the lame to walk, the deaf to hear, the leprous skin clean, the bleeding to cease, the bent and bowed to stand tall, the withered hand to unfurl, and the dead to rise, I pray You will heal my husband's body and make him whole. I praise You that You are the same yesterday and today and forever and that the miracles You performed in times past You still perform today.

> The centurion replied, "Lord, I do not deserve to have you come under my roof. But just say the word, and my servant will be healed...." Then Jesus said to the centurion, "Go! It will be done just as you believed it would." And his servant was healed at that very hour. *Matthew 8:8, 13*

Lord, I pray You will just say the word...*just say the word.* I intercede on my husband's behalf, asking You to command sickness, infirmity, and disease to leave his body. Please restore his health and renew his strength. I pray it will be done and believe it will be.

> When Jesus landed and saw a large crowd, he had compassion on them and healed their sick. *Matthew 14:14*

Lord, I ask that You have compassion on my husband and heal him totally and completely.

> Some men came, bringing to him a paralytic, carried by four of them. Since they could not get him to Jesus because of the crowd, they made an opening in the roof above Jesus and, after digging through it, lowered the mat the paralyzed man was lying on.... [Jesus said,] "I tell you, get up, take your mat and go home." He got up, took his mat and walked out in full view of them all. This amazed everyone and they praised God, saying, "We have never seen anything like this!" *Mark 2:3–4, 11–12*

Lord, just as the four men lowered their sick friend through the roof, I bring my husband before You and place him at Your feet. I ask that You heal him totally and completely so that everyone will be amazed at what You have done.

> Don't you know that you yourselves are God's temple and that God's Spirit lives in you? *1 Corinthians 3:16*

Lord, while I ask for my husband's healing, I also pray he will do his part to restore and maintain his health. Convict him to not abuse his body or ignore his health but to maintain healthy eating and exercise habits. Give him the determination to avoid anything that would harm his physical well-being. Teach him to treat his body as Your temple in which Your Spirit lives.

> And I will do whatever you ask in my name, so that the Son may bring glory to the Father. You may ask me for anything in my name, and I will do it. *John 14:13–14*

Lord, Your Word says I may ask You for anything in Your name and You will do it. I know that this means that I can ask for anything that is according to Your will and in alignment with Your purposes. With that in mind, I pray You will heal my husband totally and completely. And if it is not Your perfect will for him to be healed at this time, give us both the assurance that Your grace is sufficient, for Your power is made perfect in our weakness.

> Therefore confess your sins to each other and pray for each other so that you may be healed. *James 5:16*

Please make my husband aware of any unconfessed sin that stands in the way of his complete healing. Move him to confess his sins to a trusted friend who will pray for him so that he may be healed.

> You do not have, because you do not ask God. *James 4:2*

Lord, Your Word says that we do not have because we do not ask, so I am asking. I pray that You will heal my husband totally and completely. I pray that even now the sickness and disease will leave his body. In Jesus' name, amen.

Time for Reflection

As I prayed for my husband using the landmarks of head to toe, God surprised me with some unexpected changes in my own heart. I began to have more compassion for the struggles Steve faced every day, and I became more in tune to the Holy Spirit nudging me to intercede for him throughout the day—not just in my early morning prayer time. My senses experienced a heightened sensitivity to the sights and sounds that surrounded him, the Enemy who intended to harm him, and the people in his life who influenced him. I found myself quicker to forgive, slower to judge, and more intentional to love. Bottom line: God stirred a love for my man that went even deeper than before.

I encourage you to take some time for reflection after you have gone through the thirty days of prayer. If you are using *Praying for Your Husband from Head to Toe* with a Praying Wives group, a Bible study group, or even one other girlfriend, I encourage you to share your answers to the following questions as a way to reflect on the power of prayer in your own life.

- How has God changed your heart toward your husband as you prayed for him over the past thirty days?
- What has God shown you about your husband as you prayed for him from head to toe? Has He opened your eyes to something new that you had never seen before?
- What has God shown you about your own heart?
- What changes have you seen in your marriage?
- Have you experienced any moments of sudden glory as you have prayed for your husband—moments when God made Himself known to you in a personal way? If so, describe them.

I'd love for you to visit a special website set up just for you to share your experiences as well as your prayer requests and God's answers. Log on to www.prayingforyourhusband.com, and let's pray for each other and praise God together.

THIRTY-DAY PRAYER DARE

When I wrote the book *Becoming the Woman of His Dreams,* I interviewed hundreds of men to find out what they longed for in a wife. A common thread among the many responders is what I call the AAA Club of Marriage: adoration, appreciation, and admiration. Your man wants to know that you love him more today than you did yesterday. And he wants you to let him know it. So here's my challenge: show him.

I want to invite you to join me online for a Thirty-Day Prayer Dare. This challenge will knit together the thirty days of *Praying for Your Husband from Head to Toe* with thirty ways of letting him know just how much you love him.

Join me in the adventure by signing up at www.prayingforyour husband.com, and put a smile on your man's face.

ACKNOWLEDGMENTS

There are many women who have taught me how to pray along this journey called life. Two who have left an indelible impression on my heart and in my soul are Mary Lance Sisk and Mary Marshall Young. These two Marys sat me down when I was a young mom, taught me the principles of prayer, and led me to the throne room of God by example. Both are now enjoying eternity with the Father, and I can't wait to see them again.

A special thanks to:

Bill Jensen, for his leadership and guidance.

Laura Barker and Judy Gillispie, for their tenaciously tender editing skills.

Carie Freimuth, Lori Addicott, Amy Haddock, Johanna Inwood, Lynette Kittle, Stuart McGuiggan, Steve Reed, Tim Vanderkolk, Cara Van Meter, Rick Gingrich, and Christopher Sigfrids for using their special gifts and talents to help spread the message of *Praying for Your Husband from Head to Toe.*

My Girlfriends in God team, Gwen Smith and Mary Southerland, for encouraging me to be the best Sharon I can be.

My prayer team, for lifting me up before the Father every step of the way: Bonnie Cleveland, Bonnie Schulte, Cissy Smith, Van Walton, Cynthia Price, Dawn Lee, Debby Millhouse, Gwen Smith, Jill Archer, Karen Shiels, Kathy Mendieta, Linda Butler, Linda Eppley, Mary Southerland, and Risa Tucker.

My husband, Steve, one of God's most amazing works of art, who continues to show me what a child of God looks like.

My heavenly Father, who calls me His own.

NOTES

1. *Mounce's Complete Expository Dictionary of Old and New Testament Words* (Grand Rapids, MI: Zondervan, 2006), 332.

2. Kenneth L. Barker and John R. Kohlenberger III, *Zondervan NIV Bible Commentary,* vol. 1, (Grand Rapids, MI: Zondervan, 1994), 1006.

3. Sharon Jaynes, *What God Really Thinks About Women: Finding Your Significance Through the Women Jesus Encountered* (Eugene, OR: Harvest House, 2010), 19.

4. W. E. Vine, Merrill F. Unger, and William White Jr. *Vine's Complete Expository Dictionary of Old and New Testament Words* (Nashville, TN: Thomas Nelson, 1985), 20.

5. *Biblical Financial Study: Small Group Student Manual* (Longwood, FL: Crown Ministries, 2003), 39–40.

6. "You Choose," *Economist,* December 6, 2010, www.economist .com/node/17723028.

7. Tammy Worth, "Too Many Choices Can Tax the Brain, Research Shows," *Los Angeles Times,* March 16, 2009, http://articles .latimes.com/2009/mar/16/health/he-choices16.

8. Alina Tugend, "Too Many Choices: A Problem That Can Paralyze," *New York Times,* February 27, 2010, www.nytimes .com/2010/02/27/your-money/27shortcuts.html.

9. Vine, Unger, and White, *Vine's Expository Dictionary,* 282.

10. C. S. Lewis, *Mere Christianity* (Nashville, TN: Broadman & Holman, 1996), 96.

11. "What Percentage of Married Men Wear Wedding Rings?," ChaCha, September 25, 2011, www.chacha.com/question /what-percentage-of-married-men-wear-wedding-rings.

12. "Ring Finger," Wikipedia, http://en.wikipedia.org/wiki/Ring
    _finger; "Does the Vein in Your Ring Finger Lead to Your
    Heart?," Answers, http://wiki.answers.com/Q/Does_the_vein
    _in_your_ring_finger_lead_to_your_heart.

13. Beth Moore, *Praying God's Word: Breaking Free from Spiritual
    Strongholds* (Nashville, TN: Broadman & Holman, 2009),
    273–74.

14. Spiros Zodhiates, ed., *The Complete Word Study Dictionary: New
    Testament* (Iowa Falls, IA: World Bible, 1992), #2853, 875.

15. Theodore Roosevelt, *The Foes of Our Own Household* (New York:
    George H. Doran, 1917), 246.

ABOUT THE AUTHOR

Sharon Jaynes is an international conference speaker and best-selling author of nineteen books including *The Power of a Woman's Words, Becoming the Woman of His Dreams, Becoming a Woman Who Listens to God, I'm Not Good Enough and Other Lies Women Tell Themselves,* and *A Sudden Glory: God's Lavish Response to Your Ache for Something More.* Her books have been translated into several languages and continue to impact women for Christ all around the world.

Sharon is the cofounder of Girlfriends in God, a nondenominational conference and online ministry that seeks to cross generational, racial, and denominational boundaries to bring the body of Christ together as believers. Their online devotions reach approximately five hundred thousand subscribers daily. Sharon has coauthored two books with her ministry partners, Gwen Smith and Mary Southerland: *Trusting God* and *Knowing God by Name.* To learn more, visit www.girlfriendsingod.com.

Sharon and her husband, Steve, live in North Carolina and have one grown son, Steven.

Sharon is always honored to hear from her readers. You can connect with her via e-mail at sharon@sharonjaynes.com, follow her on Facebook at www.facebook.com/sharonjaynes, engage with her on Twitter at www.twitter.com/sharonjaynes, or pin with her at www.pinterest.com/sharonjaynes. One of her greatest joys is engaging with her readers on her blog. You can sign up at www.sharonjaynes.com.

For those who love pen and paper, you can reach her by mail at:

Sharon Jaynes

P. O. Box 725

Matthews, NC 28106

To learn more about Sharon's books, resources, and ministry, or to inquire about having Sharon speak at your event, visit www.sharon jaynes.com.

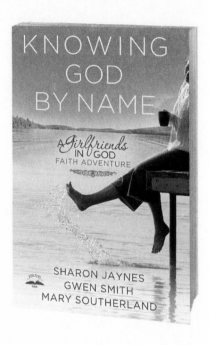